OFFENSE

The Silent Killer of Trust and Relationships

EBO DADZIE

OFFENSE

The Silent Killer of Trust and Relationships

Copyright ©2025 by Ebo Dadzie

Paperback ISBN: 978-1-965593-45-5

Published by Cornerstone Publishing

A Division of Cornerstone Creativity Group LLC
Info@thecornerstonepublishers.com
www.thecornerstonepublishers.com

Author's Contact

To book the author to speak at your next event or to order bulk copies of this book, please, use the information below:

ebodadzie1@gmail.com

Printed in the United States of America.

FOREWORD

I have had the privilege of serving alongside Pastor Ebo Dadzie over the years. We share a divine bond of love in the Spirit. Watching him navigate various relational challenges has given me unique insight into the authenticity demonstrated throughout the pages of this book.

The topic of "offenses" is crucial, especially now when our adversary, Satan, roars like a lion seeking to devour the fundamental unit of society—the family. While the weapons waging war against relationships are numerous, this book comprehensively addresses many of these challenges.

The book is well-structured and designed for practical daily application. It presents relatable everyday examples and situations, accompanied by biblical references that provide insight into God's perspective and guidance for application. The author offers practical tips to help address existing offenses and prevent new ones from developing.

This work will expand your understanding and take you on a journey to explore the subject matter deeply and practically. Pastor Ebo enables readers to systematically dissect this complex issue. His direct language encourages you to take bold steps in shutting the door to offenses while working through their emotional impact.

At its core, the book challenges readers to re-examine their relationships and confront hidden traces of rage, frustration, hurt, and pain that can serve as the foundation for a spiral of offenses. It guides you in dealing with these hidden roots and eliminating the unwanted fruits of offense from your life.

The core message will strengthen your personal relationship with God and positively influence your decisions when facing challenges in human relationships. Throughout its pages, the book emphasizes the importance of prayer, intimacy with God, Scripture, humility, effective communication, and proper godly responses based on biblical truth.

You will benefit from this journey with God through the writing of a man whose life testifies to the truths shared in these pages.

I recommend this book as a life companion for everyone, everywhere.

Apostle Victor Acquah Djan
Founder and Leader of European Missions E.V.
Staff Member, Charis Bible College, Frankfurt, Germany

DEDICATION

This book is dedicated to you, yes you, for choosing to purchase this book. You could have chosen to purchase any other book, but you chose this book and that means the world to me. For that, I am grateful.

Also to the E-squad (my wife, Emily and my kids: Eden, Elsie and Eli) who God is using to mold me into a better man.

CONTENTS

INTRODUCTION

In the web of human existence, two profound truths stand in stark contrast yet harmonious resolution. "To err is human, but to forgive is divine" captures the essence of our mortal fallibility while pointing toward a higher path of grace. This timeless wisdom finds resonance in Luke 17:1, which acknowledges the inevitability of human error: "It is impossible but that offenses will come." It simultaneously warns of the grave responsibility we bear for our actions; "But woe unto him, through whom they come!"

These complementary insights paint a nuanced picture of the human condition. We are beings capable of error and awareness of our mistakes, creatures that can comprehend the weight of our transgressions yet also aspire to the divine attribute of forgiveness. This tension between our imperfect nature and our capacity for transcendent grace forms the cornerstone of personal growth and societal healing.

Recognizing these dual truths - the certainty of human error and the possibility of divine forgiveness, creates a framework for understanding justice and mercy. It suggests that while we must acknowledge the reality of human imperfection, we are to reach beyond our natural inclinations toward a higher standard of reconciliation and grace.

Offense is an inevitable part of the human experience. We have all encountered it in our relationships with friends, family, loved ones, and fellow believers. Like ripples in a pond, hurt flows outward - those who carry wounds often inflict them on others, creating cycles of pain and misunderstanding.

An offense is complex and unpredictable. It can arise from the most unexpected sources, sometimes unintentionally through careless words or actions, other times deliberately inflicted. Its impact runs deep, and when left unaddressed, the offense can fundamentally alter the fabric of relationships.

The lingering effects of unresolved offense manifest in various ways. Once trust is damaged, it transforms simple interactions into exercises in hyper-vigilance. Those who have experienced betrayal begin to view potential allies as adversaries. Every word becomes subject to scrutiny, and every action gets filtered through the lens of past hurts. This heightened state of alertness exhausts spirit and relationships, causing people to withdraw and withhold themselves from meaningful connections.

The path to healing from an offense is crucial. Without proper healing, we risk carrying these wounds forward, allowing them to color our perceptions and limit our capacity for authentic relationships. When we remain in a state of offense, we build invisible barriers that protect us from potential hurt but prevent us from experiencing the fullness of human connection.

Learning to process and heal from an offense becomes not only a personal journey but also a necessary skill for maintaining healthy relationships. It requires us to acknowledge the pain while not allowing it to define our future interactions, to remain open to trust while being wisely discerning, and to move forward with hope rather than fear.

THEY DON'T KNOW

"Father, forgive them, for they know not what they do." These powerful words from Luke 23:34 were spoken by Jesus while being crucified, demonstrating perhaps the most profound example of forgiveness in human history.

Jesus not only taught about offense but also demonstrated forgiveness in the most difficult situation of anyone's life. This text suggests that Jesus could forgive minor offenses. He forgave when people plotted his betrayal, arrest, persecution, and crucifixion.

The phrase *"they know not what they do"* adds a new layer of depth to this teaching about forgiveness. It suggests an understanding that people's harmful actions often stem from their limitations, ignorance, or wounds. This perspective doesn't excuse the offense but offers a framework for understanding it with compassion rather than condemnation.

This verse serves as both an example and a challenge. It shows that true forgiveness is possible even in the face of the gravest offenses. It challenges us to examine our capacity to forgive when we face much lesser injuries. If such forgiveness could be offered in humanity's darkest moment, it suggests that we can find the strength to forgive in our circumstances.

Chapter 1

THE DEEPEST WOUNDS: WHEN THOSE WE TRUST BETRAY US

INTRODUCTION

The most profound wounds we endure in life rarely come from strangers or declared enemies; rather, they emerge from the unexpected betrayal of those we hold dear. This psychological phenomenon transcends mere disappointment—it constitutes a fundamental violation of our most sacred emotions. When someone we have admitted into our inner circle, someone with whom we have shared vulnerabilities and intimate moments, turns against us, the resulting anguish penetrates beyond the surface level of ordinary hurt. The severity of this pain stems from multiple factors: the implicit trust we placed in them, the emotional investment we cultivated over time, and the shattering of our foundational assumptions about relationship safety. Our psychological defenses, carefully constructed against known adversaries, stand wholly unprepared for treachery from within our circle of trust. This vulnerability to betrayal represents not just an emotional inconvenience but a profound existential challenge that forces us to reconsider the nature of trust itself.

BIBLICAL WISDOM ON BETRAYAL

"For if it was not an enemy that reproached me, then I could have borne it; neither was it he that hated me that did magnify himself against me, then I would have hidden myself from him. But it was thou, a man my equal, my guide, and my acquaintance. We took sweet counsel together and walked into the house of God in company." (Psalms 55:12–14)

"For if it was not an enemy that reproached me, then I could have borne it; neither was it he that hated me that did magnify himself against me, then I would have hidden myself from him. But it was thou, a man my equal, my guide, and my acquaintance. We took sweet counsel together and walked into the house of God in company." (Psalms 55:12–14)

These verses vividly capture the unique agony David experienced when betrayed by someone he trusted deeply. In his lament, David draws a crucial distinction: betrayal from friends wounds us far more severely than attacks from known enemies. When David writes, "If it was not an enemy," he's acknowledging a fundamental truth about human psychology—we instinctively fortify ourselves emotionally against those we identify as adversaries. We expect opposition from enemies and build protective barriers around our hearts in anticipation.

The source of David's excruciating pain becomes clear when he identifies his betrayer as "a man my equal, my guide, and my acquaintance." This wasn't a distant figure or known opponent—this was someone with whom David had shared life's intimate moments. The betrayal devastated him precisely because it came from within his circle of absolute trust, the place where he had intentionally lowered all defenses.

David's anguish intensifies as he recalls their relationship with the poignant phrase "we took sweet counsel together." This wasn't merely a casual acquaintance but someone with whom he had shared his deepest thoughts, fears, and hopes—a confidant who knew his vulnerabilities. Their relationship had transcended ordinary friendship; they had "walked into the house of God in company," sharing profound spiritual experiences and worshipping together. This spiritual dimension made the betrayal not just personally painful but spiritually traumatic, as it corrupted what David had considered sacred fellowship.

Historical context suggests this psalm likely references David's betrayal by his trusted advisor Ahithophel, who sided with Absalom's rebellion against him. The anguish in these verses reflects David's genuine historical experience while simultaneously prefiguring the betrayal Christ would later endure from Judas, one of his closest disciples. This remarkable prophetic parallel—written centuries before Jesus' birth—demonstrates why David is described as "a man after God's own heart." Through his own painful experience of betrayal, David gained spiritual insight into the suffering the Messiah would endure, creating a timeless passage that speaks to the universal human experience of being wounded by those we trust most deeply.

THE PSYCHOLOGY OF BETRAYAL

Have you ever wondered why you can dismiss certain offenses while others haunt you indefinitely? I have often expressed similar sentiments but never realized that the answer was hidden in plain sight. This scripture encapsulates the psychological reality perfectly. You can readily distance yourself from those with whom you share no significant bond—their insults fail to diminish your self-worth, their betrayal doesn't pierce your heart, and their calculated schemes leave no lasting impression. They dissipate like morning mist.

But as the scripture reveals, when a friend, family member, loved one, or close acquaintance offends you, the experience is fundamentally different. The pain becomes palpable, the wounds penetrate deeply, and the resulting scars remain both visible and significant. Our immediate internal response typically manifests as incredulity: "How could you do this to me?" followed by the anguished realization, "I never thought you capable of such actions or words." The impact is qualitatively different from offenses by strangers.

Some pain we might avoid, but other experiences of betrayal seem inevitable. Generally, those who will offend us most deeply are precisely those nearest to us, and these offenses can occur both intentionally and unintentionally.

BIBLICAL GUIDANCE FOR HANDLING OFFENSE

Left unaddressed, quarrels and misunderstandings can devastate our most cherished relationships, turning trusted confidants into perceived adversaries. In Second Timothy 2:24–26, Paul provides essential wisdom that could save our relationships from unnecessary destruction: "And the servant of God must not quarrel but be gentle to all, able to teach, patient, and humble in correcting those who are in opposition, if God perhaps will grant them repentance, so that they may know the truth, and that they may come to their senses and escape the snare of the devil."

This scripture isn't merely suggesting conflict avoidance—it's offering a transformative approach to human interaction. Paul understood that unresolved conflicts become breeding grounds for bitterness, resentment, and broken relationships. His guidance to Timothy reveals three compelling reasons why we must proactively address misunderstandings:

First, unresolved conflicts rarely dissolve on their own—they fester and expand. What begins as a minor misunderstanding can, when left unaddressed, mutate into perceived betrayal. Paul's instruction to "be gentle to all" acknowledges that our natural tendency is toward defensiveness and escalation, precisely when restraint is most needed.

Second, conflict resolution offers opportunity for growth. When Paul urges Timothy to be "able to teach," he suggests that misunderstandings provide unique teaching moments where both parties can expand their understanding. Rather than seeing differences as threats, we can view them as opportunities to develop deeper mutual comprehension.

Third, and perhaps most compelling, Paul reveals the spiritual dimension of conflict, noting that those trapped in opposition may be caught in "the snare of the devil." Unresolved conflicts create vulnerability to spiritual attack, making reconciliation not merely a social nicety but a spiritual necessity.

Consider how many relationships have been permanently damaged because one or both parties lacked the humility, patience, and gentleness Paul prescribes. The individuals who most frequently trigger our strongest emotional responses are precisely those closest to us—our friends, colleagues, family members, spouses, children, in-laws, and fellow congregants. Though Paul originally addressed "opposition" in reference to unbelievers, the principle extends universally: conflicts with those we care about require extraordinary care and intentionality.

Misunderstandings inevitably arise whenever people share proximity and relationship. However, it is our response to these tensions that determines whether they become relationship-destroying wounds or relationship-strengthening experiences. The consequences of mishandling conflicts can ripple through families for generations, while skillful resolution can transform potential division into deeper connection. This makes conflict resolution not merely a helpful skill but an essential competency for meaningful human connection.

When misunderstandings emerge, Paul's prescription is clear: approach with gentleness, communicate concerns clearly, and actively seek resolution rather than vindication. When feelings of being misunderstood arise, we must resist isolation and instead engage in transparent communication. Harboring unexpressed grievances provides fertile ground for resentment to grow. Instead, we must commit to seeking clarification with "consistent gentleness and authentic humility," precisely as Paul instructs.

A BIBLICAL FRAMEWORK FOR RESOLVING MISUNDERSTANDINGS

Paul models this approach in Second Corinthians 1:12–14: *"For our boast is this, the testimony of our conscience that we have behaved in the world, and still more toward you, with holiness and godly sincerity, not by earthly wisdom but by the grace of God. For we write you nothing but what you can read and understand; I hope you will understand fully, as you have understood in part, that you can be proud of us as we can be of you, on the day of the Lord Jesus."*

Facing a potential misunderstanding regarding his postponed visit to Corinth, Paul doesn't leave matters to chance. He proactively addresses the situation with transparency and intentionality. From his example, we can extract a practical four-step framework for resolving misunderstandings:

1. Acknowledge the misunderstanding directly:

Paul begins by recognizing the potential for misinterpretation. Similarly, we must first acknowledge when a misunderstanding exists—whether through direct conversation or thoughtful reflection. As the scripture demonstrates, no solution can address a problem whose existence remains unacknowledged.

2. Choose appropriate communication channels:

Paul writes, "For we write you nothing but what you can read and understand," showing his intentional selection of the most effective medium for clear communication. Like Paul, we must consider whether a conversation is best conducted in person, through writing, or via another medium, based on what will best facilitate understanding between the specific parties involved.

3. Communicate with deliberate clarity:

Notice how Paul emphasizes, "I hope you will understand fully, as you have understood in part." This demonstrates his commitment to precise communication that eliminates ambiguity. When addressing misunderstandings, we must articulate our thoughts with exceptional clarity, ensuring our intentions are transparent and sincere.

4. Commit to comprehensive mutual understanding:

Paul acknowledges partial understanding but strives for complete comprehension. Similarly, we must recognize that misunderstandings often stem from incomplete rather than absent understanding. Our goal should be to ensure we are fully understood—creating room for questions, clarification, and confirmation.

In practicing these biblical principles, we don't merely resolve conflicts—we transform them into opportunities for deeper connection. By following Paul's wisdom, we protect our most precious relationships from the devastation of unresolved misunderstandings and create space for healing even after betrayal has occurred.

Chapter 2

THE WOUNDED HEART: CONFRONTING DENIAL AND RESOLVING OFFENSE

·⟫⟫⟫⟫⟫⟫ • ⟪⟪⟪⟪⟪⟪·

THE MASKS WE WEAR

Over the centuries, humanity has perfected the art of deception—not merely of others, but of ourselves. We have become virtuosos at concealing truth from reality, moving through the world with choreographed smiles while carrying wounds so deep they remain invisible to the casual observer. We have mastered the architecture of appearance: carefully selecting garments that flatter our form while strategically hiding perceived imperfections, accentuating features we deem valuable, diminishing those we consider flaws. This artistry extends beyond fabric and form; we've developed sophisticated techniques for obscuring emotional scars, applying metaphorical makeup not merely to disguise what we believe diminishes us but to construct entirely new personas—carefully curated versions of ourselves designed for public consumption.

THE INSIDIOUS NATURE OF DENIAL

Perhaps the most dangerous form of self-deception emerges in the aftermath of personal offense. Those who harbor deep wounds often retreat into the shadowed sanctuary of denial—a psychological mechanism that appears protective but ultimately proves corrosive.

When someone wounds us deeply, acknowledging that wound requires admitting vulnerability—conceding that another human being possessed sufficient power to penetrate our emotional defenses. This recognition threatens our carefully constructed illusion of invulnerability. So instead, we engage in elaborate psychological theater, pretending indifference while secretly nurturing our injuries.

"I'm fine," we insist with practiced nonchalance, even as invisible hemorrhaging continues beneath the surface.

"It doesn't bother me," we declare convincingly, while internally rehearsing the offensive words or actions with obsessive precision.

"I've moved past it," we assure others, while privately constructing elaborate mental arguments against our offenders.

This denial operates on multiple levels of consciousness. At its most superficial, we present a façade of composure to the world, concealing any evidence of distress. Deeper still, we may convince ourselves that we have transcended the offense through spiritual maturity or emotional fortitude. Yet in the subterranean chambers of our hearts, the wound festers unaddressed.

The tragedy of denial lies in its fundamentally counterproductive nature. By refusing to acknowledge our pain, we paradoxically grant it greater power over us. The unexamined wound becomes a hidden influence, subtly affecting our attitudes, decisions, and relationships. We develop invisible triggers that, when activated, produce reactions disproportionate to present circumstances—emotional echoes of unresolved past injuries.

Denial manifests in myriad forms, each with its own distinctive characteristics:

13

1. **Intellectual Denial** occurs when we rationalize away the significance of the offense. "It wasn't that serious," we tell ourselves. "Anyone would have done the same in their position." We construct elaborate justifications for the offender's behavior while refusing to acknowledge the legitimate pain it caused us.

2. **Spiritual Denial** hides behind religious language and concepts. "I've forgiven them already," we claim prematurely, without having processed our genuine feelings. We weaponize spiritual concepts to bypass emotional processing, mistaking suppression for authentic spiritual growth.

3. **Temporal Denial** uses time as a shield. "That happened years ago—I'm over it now," we insist, even as unprocessed emotions continue influencing our present reality. We confuse the passage of time with genuine healing, failing to recognize that unaddressed wounds do not heal spontaneously but merely change form.

4. **Comparative Denial** minimizes our pain through contrast. "Others have suffered far worse," we remind ourselves. While perspective has value, using others' greater suffering to invalidate our own emotional experiences prevents authentic processing and resolution.

5. **Social Denial** manifests when we maintain superficial relationships with those who have wounded us. We engage in polite conversation, exchange pleasantries, and participate in shared activities while carefully avoiding any acknowledgment of the unresolved offense. This creates a peculiar dynamic where both parties tacitly agree to interact within careful boundaries, never addressing the elephant in the room.

The insidiousness of denial lies in its ability to masquerade as strength. Our culture often celebrates those who "don't let things bother them" or who "move on quickly" from offense. We equate emotional resilience with the ability to suppress pain rather than process it. This cultural narrative reinforces our natural tendency toward denial, creating a perfect storm where external validation meets internal resistance to confronting painful truths.

Yet denial exacts a tremendous cost. Research in psychoneuroimmunology has demonstrated that unprocessed emotional trauma affects not only our psychological well-being but our physical health. Chronic denial correlates with elevated stress hormones, compromised immune function, and increased inflammatory responses. The energy required to maintain denial depletes resources that could otherwise support creativity, joy, and authentic connection.

Moreover, denial prevents genuine reconciliation. When we refuse to acknowledge how deeply someone has wounded us, we cannot engage in the honest dialogue necessary for relationship restoration. Instead, we create superficial peace—a fragile détente that preserves social harmony at the expense of authentic healing.

THE FRUITS OF OFFENSE

The Holy Spirit produces fruit in our lives, but offense, too, bears its distinctive harvest—bitter fruit that reveals the presence of unresolved wounds. Recognizing these manifestations allows us to identify resentment we may be harboring, often unconsciously, in the hidden chambers of our hearts.

This self-examination is crucial because many believers experience repeated defeats in the battle with offense precisely due to ignorance about the enemy's tactical approach. Scripture warns us plainly: "My people are destroyed for lack of knowledge; because you have rejected knowledge, I reject you from being a priest to me. And since you have forgotten the law of your God, I also will forget your children" (Hosea 4:6).

This principle applies profoundly to the matter of offense. Lack of understanding about how offense operates destroys relationships, ministries, and spiritual effectiveness. As those called to function as "kings and priests" in God's kingdom, ignorance about these matters proves particularly devastating. The sobering warning that rejection of knowledge leads to divine rejection underscores the seriousness of this issue.

A timeless maxim captures this truth perfectly: "The strength of the enemy lies in your ignorance." The adversary's power diminishes proportionally as our understanding increases. Scripture affirms this principle when it declares that "we are not ignorant of the devil's schemes" (2 Corinthians 2:11). Some translations render these as "designs" or "devices"—strategic plans crafted to undermine our spiritual effectiveness.

We strip the enemy of power through knowledge acquisition, ensuring we operate from a position of advantage rather than disadvantage. Yet often we trust our feelings so completely that we forget how effectively the enemy can weaponize emotions against us.

This battle engages two ancient spirits: God and the adversary. Their antiquity means nothing about human nature remains hidden from either. They understand us far better than we comprehend them. Wisdom, therefore, dictates heeding divine counsel delivered through God's chosen vessels. We must embrace truth rather than persisting in denial.

If you recognize any of the following responses toward an individual, situation, organization, or church, you are likely contending with unresolved offense:

- Persistent strife

- Lingering bitterness

- Intentionally ignoring certain people

- Disproportionate anger

- Hardened hatred

- Deliberately avoiding specific individuals

- Withdrawing from community because of issues with one person

- Questioning established relationships

- The subtle yet revealing eye roll

- Hidden heart palpitations when encountering certain individuals

This list merely scratches the surface. Take a moment for honest self-reflection, identifying your typical reactions when encountering someone who has wounded you, even if those reactions don't appear above. Remember: denying or ignoring pain caused by offense doesn't constitute healing. Sweeping issues under the rug doesn't truly clean the room—it merely conceals the dirt until the covering is removed. And this analogy doesn't even begin to address what lurks in deeper hiding places—beneath the bed or within closed closets.

The time has come for thorough spiritual housecleaning. Too many festering issues remain hidden in dark corners of our hearts, requiring illumination and cleansing.

> *"We cannot dive deep into God and the things of God while carrying this heavy luggage of offense."*

THE PROGRESSION OF DENIAL

Living in denial resembles ignoring a seemingly minor physical ailment—perhaps a muscle twitch or slight sprain. Initially, it presents as negligible discomfort that seems tolerable. Yet that same "insignificant" issue, when neglected or improperly addressed, often transforms into a chronic condition with far-reaching consequences.

Many of us navigate life with hearts harboring unacknowledged pain because the original wounds remain unresolved. We become hypersensitive, easily triggered by the slightest provocation from friends, family members, and the double-edged blessing-curse of social media. The smallest comment or perceived slight activates our unhealed wounds, producing reactions disproportionate to the current stimulus.

Denial progresses through predictable stages, each more destructive than the last:

1. **Stage One: Minimization** - We acknowledge something occurred but downplay its significance. "It wasn't that bad," we tell ourselves, even as our emotional response indicates otherwise.

2. **Stage Two: Compartmentalization** - We isolate the offense from other aspects of life, creating psychological partitions that prevent integration. "I don't think about it except when I see them," we claim, failing to recognize how the unresolved issue influences our broader emotional landscape.

3. **Stage Three: Projection** - We begin attributing negative intentions to the offender beyond the original offense. "They always meant to hurt me," we conclude, reinterpreting past interactions through the lens of our pain.

4. **Stage Four: Generalization** - We extend our negative feelings beyond the offender to others who share certain characteristics. "You can never trust people like that," we decide, allowing one wound to alter our entire approach to relationships.

5. **Stage Five: Identity Formation -** We incorporate the offense into our self-concept. "I'm just someone who gets betrayed," we determine, allowing victimhood to become a central aspect of our identity.

For those entrenched in denial, I prescribe a sincere moment of truth with the Holy Spirit. This sacred encounter requires two keys: transparent vulnerability and unflinching honesty.

Can God reconcile your external expressions—your words and gestures—with the authentic contents of your heart? Many have grown adept at verbal misdirection, saying one thing while meaning something entirely different, maintaining elaborate façades that deceive others and sometimes even themselves.

Consider David, who approached God with radical transparency in Psalm 139:23: "Search me, O God, and know my heart; try me, and know my thoughts." This represents one of the most vulnerable prayers recorded in scripture. Imagine standing before an omniscient Creator and inviting complete examination. David understood that nothing in his heart remained hidden from divine perception. He embraced the fundamental truth that nothing escapes God's sight.

Most shrink from such vulnerability, fearing what might be uncovered. Yet divine revelation of our sin, followed by healing, ultimately serves us better than remaining ignorant until destruction overtakes us. Like Isaiah, who cried, "Woe is me, for I am undone; I am a man of unclean lips," we benefit from being "undone" before God—experiencing honest revelation of our true condition in divine sight.

Like someone requiring life-saving open-heart surgery, we desperately need thorough, transformative spiritual examination. The temporary pain of honest self-confrontation ultimately leads to lasting healing that superficial denial can never provide.

O God, help us. Undo us. We have concealed our authentic condition beneath layers of self-righteousness, pretense, hypocrisy, and self-imposed naiveté.

RESOLVING QUARRELS

1. Learn to Communicate with Crystalline Clarity

Effective conflict resolution begins with communication characterized by crystal clarity. Express thoughts and emotions without ambiguity, employing "I" statements that claim your experience rather than accusatory language that escalates defensiveness. Specificity matters—identify precisely what troubled you rather than resorting to sweeping generalizations that create space for misinterpretation. Ensure alignment between your words and intended message, avoiding subtle hints or expecting others to decipher unstated meanings. Clear communication establishes the essential foundation upon which effective conflict resolution can be built.

2. Embrace Discomfort as the Price of Growth

Accepting discomfort constitutes a non-negotiable element of conflict resolution. These conversations were never designed for ease; they inherently generate tension. Embrace the disquieting nature of addressing difficult subjects, recognizing that genuine development typically occurs beyond the boundaries of your comfort zone. Understand that temporary uneasiness represents a modest price compared to the burden of carrying perpetual resentment. This awareness can mobilize you to confront challenging moments directly rather than avoiding them. Healing relationships frequently requires walking through awkward or uncomfortable interactions rather than circumventing them.

3. Abandon Defensive Postures

To resolve conflicts effectively, prioritize listening with genuine intent to understand rather than mentally rehearsing your counterarguments while others speak. Receive criticism without rushing to justify yourself. Accept responsibility for your contribution to the conflict and create space for others to express their perspectives without interruption. Resist the instinctive urge to protect your ego or reputation. Instead, remain receptive to difficult truths about yourself and your actions, understanding that defensiveness blocks the path to authentic resolution.

4. Relinquish Rigid Opinions — Consider Alternative Perspectives

Acknowledge that your viewpoint represents one valid perspective among many, not the exclusive truth. This mindset creates space for genuine resolution. Demonstrate intellectual flexibility by remaining open to perspective shifts when presented with new information—an indication of maturity and wisdom rather than weakness. Seek to understand the foundational reasoning behind divergent viewpoints, respecting their validity even amid disagreement. Focus energy on discovering common ground rather than magnifying differences, as this approach constructs bridges rather than walls between people.

THE THREE CRITICAL DIMENSIONS OF CONFLICT RESOLUTION

1. Our Resistance to Accountability

Our natural aversion to responsibility frequently obstructs conflict resolution. We instinctively avoid situations where our actions might face scrutiny, allowing fear of confronting our mistakes to deter us from pursuing resolution. Pride creates barriers that prevent acknowledgment of error, while reluctance to face consequences keeps us trapped in destructive cycles of denial and avoidance. Breaking this pattern requires the courage to embrace accountability as the pathway to freedom rather than a threat to be avoided.

2. Confronting Personal Weaknesses

Acknowledging personal flaws demands genuine self-reflection and unflinching honesty. Commit to truthfulness about areas requiring improvement and dedicate yourself to character development rather than conflict avoidance. Understanding how your particular weaknesses contribute to relational discord can motivate concrete steps toward growth and maturity. This process transforms conflict from merely painful experiences into opportunities for profound personal development.

3. Engaging in Courageous Conversations

Embrace difficult discussions as catalysts for growth and relationship strengthening. Avoiding important topics due to discomfort allows issues to fester and intensify over time. Commit to addressing concerns before they metastasize into larger problems. Creating space for honest dialogue, despite its challenges, demonstrates genuine investment in the relationship. Facing hard conversations builds stronger, more authentic connections with others. Healthy relationships thrive on transparent communication, making these discussions essential despite their inherent difficulty.

INTEGRATING THESE PRINCIPLES

These elements work synergistically to foster healthier relationships, resolve conflicts effectively, and stimulate both personal and spiritual growth. By cultivating honest communication and addressing minor issues before escalation, we develop more meaningful and enduring connections. Implementation requires humility and patience, understanding that developing these capacities represents an ongoing journey requiring consistent practice and dedication.

"Your perspective influences your perception."

A LESSON ON PERSPECTIVE

Your particular vantage point inevitably shapes your judgment. However, genuine growth requires appreciating and integrating different perspectives. Others frequently notice elements you've overlooked from your position. Consider the analogy of driving— another vehicle may occupy your blind spot, invisible to you despite being physically present. That vehicle remains perfectly visible to passengers in your rear seat or drivers in adjacent lanes. Failing to look carefully or ignoring their warnings courts disaster.

Your blind spot exists in full view of observers positioned differently. This principle applies not only to driving but to conflict resolution, personal growth, and spiritual development. The limitations of your perspective don't negate the validity of what others can see clearly from their vantage point.

True wisdom begins with recognizing the inherent limitations of individual perspective and embracing the complementary insights others provide. This approach transforms potential conflicts from zero-sum disputes into collaborative explorations that expand everyone's understanding.

Chapter 3

GUARD YOUR HEART: A SHIELD AGAINST OFFENSE

The heart—that profound center of our emotional and spiritual being—requires vigilant protection. Just as a fortress guards its most valuable treasures, we must guard our hearts against the subtle invasion of offense, which, once allowed entry, circulates through our entire being, affecting our thoughts, actions, and relationships. In Proverbs 4:23, we find wisdom that has stood the test of time: *"Guard your heart with all diligence, for out of it flow the issues of life."* This ancient counsel reminds us that what we allow into our hearts ultimately shapes who we become.

When offense takes residence in our hearts, it doesn't remain isolated. Like blood flowing through our physical heart to every part of our body, offense spreads through our spiritual and emotional framework, contaminating our perspective, tainting our relationships, and distorting our character. To live lives of integrity, peace, and purpose, we must become vigilant gatekeepers of what we allow into this sacred space.

THE HEART'S PROFOUND INFLUENCE

"The heart is deceitful above all things and desperately wicked: who can know it?" (Jeremiah 17:9).

Martin Luther King Jr. said, "Do not judge a man by the color of his skin but by the content of his heart." Jesus taught, "It is not what goes into a man that defiles him, but what comes out of his mouth." These profound statements reveal an essential truth: we are judged by the content of our hearts. Our hearts define our character and personality. We are characterized by what resides in our hearts—justified by it and, in the same way, potentially condemned by it.

Proverbs 4:23 instructs us, "Guard your heart with all diligence, for out of it flow the issues of life." Consider the heart in its physical function within the circulatory system—everything that enters the chambers must be pumped out to reach the entire body. Whatever flows into the heart inevitably flows out. With this understanding, we must recognize that once offense enters our hearts, it circulates through every fiber of our being. We must be mindful of what we allow to take residence in our hearts because it shapes who we are and how we respond to situations and life in general.

HOW DO WE GUARD OUR HEARTS?

To protect this vital center of our being:

- Be mindful of what you listen to

- Be careful of what you see or watch

- Meditate on godly things

- Do not listen to ungodly counsel

- Do not have close associations with those who lead you astray

- Be mindful of your confessions

These practices help us guard our hearts and live pure lives aligned with divine purpose.

As Philippians 4:8 reminds us: "Finally, brethren, whatsoever things are true, whatsoever things are honest, whatsoever things are just, whatsoever things are pure, whatsoever things are lovely, whatsoever things are of good report, if there be any virtue, and if there be any praise, think on these things."

THE BATTLEFIELD OF THE MIND AND THE ALCHEMY OF THOUGHT

When you catch yourself drifting into thoughts displeasing to God, reject them immediately and decisively. In those critical moments when darkness seeks to establish a foothold in your consciousness, speak aloud to yourself—let your voice become the sword that severs the ties to destructive thinking patterns. This practice is not merely helpful; it is essential for the soul that seeks to walk in light and truth.

The mind, that magnificent frontier of human experience, stands as the ultimate battlefield where good and evil wage their eternal war, where light and darkness dance their ancient dance of dominance. It is here, in this sacred chamber of consciousness, that our destiny takes shape, for the mind is truly the seat of the soul. Our beliefs shape our reality with astonishing precision—if we believe we are weak, that weakness flows like a subtle poison through our bodies; if we believe we are strong, that strength courses through our veins like divine fire, empowering every cell and sinew.

By merely contemplating strength, we summon it into being. The ancient wisdom rings eternally true: "As a man thinketh, so is he."

Consider, if you will, the mind as a master brewer's vessel sacred barrel where thoughts ferment and mature. Just as the vintner knows that the finest wines emerge from barrels carefully tended over years, allowing time and silence to work their mysterious alchemy, so too do our thoughts develop potency with dwelling. The patient brewmaster does not rush this sacred process but understands that excellence demands time. Our thoughts, like these brewing elixirs, develop over time, either into nourishing wisdom or toxic bitterness.

The longer a thought remains in our minds—whether virtuous or vile—the more deeply it influences the very essence of who we are. When we choose to dwell upon that which is honest, true, pure, and godly, these virtues bloom within us like exotic gardens, transforming our character from the inside out. This profound principle holds the key not only to spiritual vitality but to mental and emotional wellness that modern psychology is only beginning to comprehend. This scriptural truth stands as a lighthouse, capable of guiding countless souls from the treacherous shores of anxiety, depression, and fear toward the haven of mental wholeness.

Yet beware, for this same principle works in reverse with terrifying efficiency. When offense is granted sanctuary in our thoughts, it doesn't remain static—it grows with frightening momentum, sinking roots deep into the soil of our consciousness, becoming ever more resistant to the healing balm of forgiveness. Like invasive vines that strangle a garden of virtue, nursed grievances eventually overrun the mind that harbors them.

And what of our emotions, those powerful currents that sweep through the landscape of our hearts? Make no mistake—we stand at our most vulnerable when these tides control our actions. Emotions serve divine purposes, allowing us to experience the rich tapestry of human experience and connect with the world God has created. In transcendent moments, our emotions may even become sacred vessels, surrendered to the Divine for higher purposes. Yet we must recognize a fundamental truth: emotions make wonderful servants but terrible masters.

We must maintain vigilant mindfulness in our relationships with both God and our fellow travelers on this earthly journey, ensuring that emotions—however powerful or persuasive—never seize the wheel of our decision-making. For when feelings ascend to the throne of our choices, faith invariably retreats to the shadows, and God's perfect wisdom is eclipsed by the flickering light of our momentary passions.

Envision, if you will, the mind and heart as twin chambers of a sacred temple, connected by an invisible ladder of extraordinary significance. This mysterious passageway creates a perpetual exchange between thought and feeling, intellect and intuition, reason and passion. Like two sovereign nations with open borders and continuous commerce, what enters one realm inevitably influences the other. The thoughts you entertain in your mind descend with remarkable ease into the chambers of your heart, coloring your affections and shaping your desires. Likewise, what you cherish in your heart ascends effortlessly into your mind, framing your perceptions and directing your attention.

Therefore, with all vigilance and sacred determination, guard your heart and govern your thoughts, understanding that they exist in perpetual communion, shaping each other and, ultimately, crafting the masterpiece—or tragedy—of your life's journey. By standing as a faithful sentinel at the gates of your consciousness, rejecting the poison of offense and embracing the nectar of virtue, you create within yourself a sanctuary where peace that passes understanding, wisdom that transcends human limitation, and divine purpose can flourish in magnificent abundance. In this sacred vigilance lies not restriction but true freedom, the liberty to become all that your Creator intended when He first breathed life into your soul.

Chapter 4

THE ROOT OF OFFENSE

UNFORGIVENESS: THE FERTILE SOIL OF BITTERNESS

The root of offense is unforgiveness. While offenses are an inevitable part of life, unforgiveness is what sustains them and allows them to grow into deep-seated bitterness. When we refuse to forgive, we nurture the initial hurt, transforming a momentary wound into a persistent source of pain that infiltrates every aspect of our being.

Jesus addressed this profound truth directly: "But if you forgive not men their trespasses, neither will your Father forgive your trespasses" (Matthew 6:15). These words carry both warning and wisdom—showing that our unwillingness to forgive others creates a spiritual barrier that prevents us from experiencing God's forgiveness in our own lives.

Understanding the foundation of offense helps us recognize that while we cannot control whether an offense comes, we can control how we respond to it. By addressing unforgiveness at its root level and maintaining a heart of forgiveness, we can prevent offense from establishing a stronghold in our lives. The strength of an offense lies not in the initial hurt but in our response to it. When we choose forgiveness, we break the foundation of offense and build instead on the foundation of God's love and grace.

SPIRITUAL IMMATURITY AND OFFENSE

Mark 4:16–17 provides profound insight into how offense affects the spiritually immature: *"And these are they likewise which are sown on stony ground; who, when they have heard the word, immediately receive it with gladness; and have no root in themselves, and so endure but for a time: afterward, when affliction or persecution arises for the word's sake, immediately they are offended."*

This passage reveals that those without deep spiritual roots are easily offended when facing challenges or persecution. Like plants without strong roots, they lack the foundation to withstand difficulties. Their spiritual growth is stunted because they have not developed the resilience that comes from being deeply rooted in Christ.

The term "root" brings to mind a plant or tree. One definition of a root is the part of a plant that attaches itself to the ground or growing medium, typically underground, conveying water and nourishment to the rest of the plant. It can also mean the cause or origin of something. In this chapter, we address both meanings: root as the foundation and the source of our responses to offense.

Whenever we are offended, our feelings are hurt, and we are wounded internally, which is why we feel the pain. Offense can arise from a violation of our personality, an infringement of boundaries, defamation of character, an invasion of personal space, or a complete disregard of authority. One of the easiest ways to offend or be offended is through remarks deemed derogatory, insensitive, unkind, or thoughtless.

Caution is necessary when dealing with highly sensitive people. They are like flammable gases; you never know when they might explode at the slightest appearance of heat or fire. The least remark could lead to irritation.

Many such individuals have little to no sense of humor, requiring everything to be done carefully and thoughtfully, or they will interpret it negatively.

ROOTED AND GROUNDED IN LOVE

"That Christ may dwell in your hearts by faith; that you, being rooted and grounded in love, may be able to comprehend with all saints what is the breadth, and length, and depth, and height; and to know the love of Christ, which passes knowledge" (Ephesians 3:17–19).

In this letter, Apostle Paul makes an emphatic appeal through prayer, expressing the heartfelt need for Christians to be rooted and grounded in love. Everything we do must be characterized by love. Paul demonstrates the dimensions of Christ's love by relating it to breadth, length, depth, and height, revealing the immeasurable extent of God's love for all believers. This is the kind of love we are expected to live by and extend to others— even those who have wounded us.

Consider this botanical analogy: every plant has two vascular tissues, the xylem and the phloem. For this discussion, let us focus on the xylem, which is the primary means of transporting water and minerals from the roots to the leaves. This tissue connects to the roots, the source and foundation of the plant. Whatever the roots absorb from their immediate surroundings is delivered to the rest of the plant. Similarly, whatever we are rooted in gets transported into our whole system. What do you choose to be rooted and grounded in? I hope you choose love, not offense.

When we are rooted in unforgiveness, bitterness flows through our entire being like toxic nutrients through a plant's vascular system. But when we are rooted in love and forgiveness, we draw spiritual nourishment that sustains health and growth, even in challenging circumstances.

THE WICKEDNESS OF OFFENSE

Matthew 24:10 highlights the progressive nature of offense in the context of the end times: "And then shall many be offended, and shall betray one another, and shall hate one another."

This passage is part of Jesus' discourse on the signs of the end of the age, emphasizing a spiritual and moral breakdown in the last days. The verse reveals how offense can lead to increasingly destructive behavior, starting with being offended—a seemingly minor emotional reaction—and spiraling into deeper, more harmful actions.

This progression unfolds in three devastating stages:

First is **being offended**. This initial stage is the emotional response to perceived wrongs or disagreements. In the end times, people will become easily offended, perhaps due to unmet expectations, personal grievances, or moral challenges in the world. Today's culture of offense, where people often feel hurt or slighted by words or actions, reflects this stage.

Next comes **betrayal**. When an offense is not resolved and allowed to fester, it can lead to broken relationships. Betrayal represents a deeper level of personal violation, where trust is broken, and individuals turn on one another. This applies not only to personal relationships but also to societal dynamics, where loyalties shift and alliances are broken due to unresolved offenses.

Finally, unchecked offense culminates in **hatred**. Hatred is the culmination of emotional and relational decay, where grievances deepen into animosity. It breaks down community and love, leaving a society marked by division and strife.

This progression warns against harboring offense and unresolved anger. Jesus' words remind us that without reconciliation and forgiveness, what begins as a simple offense can escalate into serious consequences. Spiritually, this serves as a call to avoid holding grudges, to forgive one another, and to seek peace, lest we fall into these destructive patterns.

ISOLATION VERSUS INTERVENTION

"A brother offended is harder to be won than a strong city, and their contentions are like the bars of a castle" (Proverbs 18:19).

In an ideal world, a brother—or, for equality's sake, a sister—should neither be offended nor offend. However, Jesus acknowledged that offenses are inevitable, saying in Luke 17:1, "It is impossible but that offenses will come." Other translations describe offense as a temptation to sin or a stumbling block that causes someone to fall. The contentions of an offended brother are indeed like the bars of a castle, making reconciliation as difficult as navigating a maze without a map. Breaking through their arguments feels impossible because their minds are already made up.

It is riveting to consider an offended person as a strong city. Ancient cities like Athens, Jericho, Babylon, and Nineveh were distinguished for their impressive defenses, including towering walls and almost impenetrable gates. In Joshua 2:15, Rahab, a woman of questionable repute, hid the spies sent by Joshua to survey the Promised Land, a land inhabited by giants. While visiting a prostitute's house is rarely advisable, in this case, it served the critical purpose of avoiding detection and potentially saving lives.

Interestingly, Rahab's house was built on the wall of a strong city. Immerse yourself in this passage and picture the sight of a house built within such a wall. If such a city is easier to conquer than winning over an offended person, then our work is indeed cut out for us. Only the Holy Spirit is qualified to break through the walls of isolation, division, partition, and seclusion.

Marginalizing people to prevent future hurt is not the solution. Instead of choosing isolation, let us pursue intervention. By facing fears, worries, and anxieties head-on, we can engage in difficult conversations to truly hear one another. As 2 Corinthians 5:19 declares, "God is reconciling the world to himself in Christ, not counting people's sins against them. And he has committed to us the message of reconciliation."

We must pursue this ministry of reconciliation with diligence. While the task may seem daunting, the potential results should inspire us to at least give it a chance. Will we succeed in reconciling with everyone? Perhaps not. But is it possible? I believe so, through the power of forgiveness that breaks the root of bitterness and allows genuine healing to begin.

BREAKING THE ROOT OF BITTERNESS

Hebrews 12:15 warns us to *"See to it that no one falls short of the grace of God and that no bitter root grows up to cause trouble and defile many."* This powerful metaphor of a bitter root illustrates how unforgiveness, when left unaddressed, grows beneath the surface of our lives, eventually producing toxic fruit that affects not only ourselves but those around us.

When we allow unforgiveness to take root in our hearts, it creates a foundation for bitterness that spreads throughout our entire being. Like a poisonous root system that extends far beyond what is visible above ground, unforgiveness silently expands its influence, affecting our thoughts, emotions, relationships, and even our physical health.

The bitter root of unforgiveness manifests in various ways:

1. **Emotional distress**: Chronic anger, anxiety, depression, and emotional volatility

2. **Mental fixation**: Obsessive thoughts about the offense and the offender

3. **Distorted perception**: Viewing life through the lens of past hurts

4. **Relationship damage**: Creating barriers to intimacy and trust

5. **Spiritual deterioration**: Hindering our relationship with God and others

6. **Physical symptoms**: Stress-related illness and compromised immune function

To break this destructive cycle, we must address unforgiveness at its root. This requires honest self-examination, acknowledging our hurt without justifying our bitterness, and making the conscious choice to forgive—not once, but as many times as necessary until the root is fully extracted.

True forgiveness is not a feeling but a decision, often made against the current of our emotions. It's a choice to release the offender from the debt we feel they owe us, to surrender our right to retaliation, and to allow God's healing grace to transform our pain.

When we uproot unforgiveness and plant ourselves instead in the soil of God's love and grace, we create the conditions for genuine healing and spiritual growth. The same energy once devoted to nursing our wounds can now be channeled into cultivating the fruit of the Spirit—love, joy, peace, patience, kindness, goodness, faithfulness, gentleness, and self-control (Galatians 5:22-23).

Remember, forgiveness doesn't excuse the offense or deny the hurt. Rather, it frees us from carrying the burden of bitterness so we can move forward in wholeness and peace. By addressing unforgiveness at its root, we prevent offense from defining our lives and instead allow God's love to shape our character and restore our joy.

Chapter 5

PUT THE PAST BEHIND YOU

Like many others, I was gravely disappointed by the news of the breakup of a famous pop culture duo known for their unique ability to sing and dance. After years of success, they decided to part ways. They had shared a womb, encroaching on each other's spaces but never getting tangled by their respective umbilical cords. Of course, one could argue that babies do not think as adults do and cannot resonate with adult emotions.

This story reminds me of an ancient narrative of fraternal twins recorded in the Bible. You may have guessed that I am talking about Jacob and Esau. Let us turn to the book of Genesis and explore their profound story.

The Bible recounts that the two babies jostled within their mother, prompting her to ask, "Why is this happening to me?" So she went to inquire of the Lord, and in Genesis 25:23, God answered her: Glory! Hallelujah! That excites me! Those who inquire will hear Him speak. The Lord said to her, "Two nations are in your womb, and two peoples from within you will be separated; one people will be stronger than the other, and the older will serve the younger." One might expect the story of the first recorded twins in Scripture to be more exhilarating, but it carries profound lessons that still speak to us today.

Esau was a hunter, and Jacob was possibly a tent maker. Esau willingly traded his birthright and was later deprived of his blessing as the firstborn by his brother—with the unflinching support of the woman who conceived and delivered both (their mother). Genesis 27:41 tells us that Esau, in his bitterness, contemplated killing Jacob after the days of mourning for their father were over. Jacob fled with nothing but a blessing.

As time passed—days turning into weeks, weeks into months, and months into years—both brothers embarked on lifelong journeys, all under the watchful eye of God, whose divine purpose unfolded through their lives. Then came a pivotal moment, a Kairos moment, for their reunion.

Immerse yourself in the Scripture as this scene unfolds. Notice Jacob, the one blessed with the covenant, bowing down seven times until he came near to his brother (a detail we will explore in a later chapter). But for now, pay attention to Esau's response. Genesis 33:4 tells us: "Esau ran to meet Jacob and embraced him; he threw his arms around his neck and kissed him. And they wept."

It is remarkable to witness the stark contrast in disposition from a man who once sought to kill his brother now running to embrace him. This act expressed love, a longing for connection, and an indication that he had missed his brother. Esau had been robbed of his birthright and struggled through much of his life. Surely, there were moments when he wished for his brother's companionship, times when he longed for his father's blessing, and countless other moments when he needed family to share his burdens.

Yet, despite all the reasons he had to hold a grudge, Esau chose reconciliation over resentment. He looked past the bitterness, the pain, and the injustices, and embraced his brother. This act of grace and forgiveness speaks volumes about the strength of character required to overcome the past and restore what was broken.

PARENTS WITH PREFERRED CHILDREN

"And the boys grew: and Esau was a cunning hunter, a man of the field; and Jacob was a plain man, dwelling in tents. And Isaac loved Esau because he did eat of his venison, but Rebekah loved Jacob." (Genesis 25:27-34)

This passage reveals the complex family dynamics between Isaac, Rebekah, and their twin sons, Esau and Jacob.

Esau is described as a skilled hunter and outdoorsman, representing a more physically robust and traditionally masculine archetype, while Jacob is characterized as a "plain man" who dwells in tents, suggesting a more domestic and contemplative nature.

The text highlights parental favoritism: Isaac's love for Esau is directly linked to his appreciation for the game Esau brings home, while Rebekah's preference for Jacob stems from what God told her about her two sons: *"And the Lord said unto her, Two nations are in thy womb, and two manner of people shall be separated from thy bowels; and the one people shall be stronger than the other people; and the elder shall serve the younger."*

When her time to deliver arrived, behold, there were twins in her womb. God had revealed a mystery to Rebekah, the mother of the two boys. She had insight into their future. At this moment, we are unsure if Isaac had any knowledge of this revelation or whether Rebekah informed him. Two things are clear: both parents had preferences. Isaac preferred Esau because of what he would gain, but Rebekah had a preference because of what God had said.

Parental preferences can profoundly impact children's psychological development and self-perception. They can have psychological, developmental, and potential lifelong effects. Parental favoritism can deeply traumatize children, causing significant psychological and developmental challenges. When parents demonstrate clear favoritism, children internalize complex emotional messages about their inherent worth and potential.

The less-favored child often develops significant self-esteem issues, experiencing persistent feelings of inadequacy and rejection. These emotional wounds can manifest in lifelong patterns of seeking validation, struggling with interpersonal relationships, and battling internal narratives of unworthiness.

Psychologically, children interpret parental preferences as a direct measure of their value. This perception can dramatically shape identity formation, career choices, and emotional responses to future relationships. The child may develop compensatory behaviors, attempting to gain approval or overachieve to prove their significance.

This preferential treatment sets the stage for future familial conflict, particularly regarding inheritance and birthright.

The contrast between the two sons foreshadows the significant narrative of rivalry, deception, and eventual reconciliation that unfolds in the biblical account of Jacob and Esau.

Families have been shattered because of preferential treatment. Having preferences has driven wedges between siblings.

Irrespective of blessings, skills, talents, gifts, abilities, natural tendencies, intelligence, resemblance, careers, money, or fame, parents must never have preferences.

SIBLING RIVALRY

This is the story of a man loved by his father but hated by his brothers through no fault of his own. Joseph, the man in question, had two dreams. In the first, the sun, moon, and stars bowed to him; in the second, his brothers' sheaves bowed to his. These dreams, which alluded to Joseph's future dominion over his parents and siblings, infuriated his brothers. They plotted to kill him, though their father took notice of the dreams.

While wandering in the plains under the scorching sun, Joseph found his brothers in Dothan, guided by a stranger. His elder brothers, failing in their fundamental duty to love and protect him, conspired to destroy him.

While God had revealed His plan to deliver Israel from an impending famine that could destroy His people, the enemy was discreetly working to thwart this plan of redemption. If evil had succeeded in manipulating the brothers to kill Joseph, Israel would have been wiped out by the famine. However, God intervened, providing a way of escape by orchestrating Joseph's journey from Israel to Egypt. Through divine providence, Joseph's survival and eventual elevation were ensured.

Joseph was cast into a dry pit while his brothers callously sat down to eat. One must wonder: Did they feel no remorse? Were they not raised in a godly home? How do you cast your own brother into a pit and then sit down comfortably to eat while deliberating and orchestrating his death? It's unfathomable. I can only imagine the thoughts racing through Joseph's mind as he overhears their conversation, listening to the negotiation where his own siblings plan to trade him to merchants of foreign origin. Despite the betrayal and the pain of his plight, Joseph remained silent—he did not utter a word in protest.

Joseph is, without question, a foreshadowing of Jesus, offering us a prophetic glimpse into the future. Just as Joseph was sold as a commodity, our Messiah, Jesus, would later be betrayed and sold for thirty pieces of silver. This parallel is a profound reminder of God's redemptive plan woven throughout history.

Isaiah 53:7 states, *"He was oppressed, and he was afflicted, yet he opened not His mouth. He is brought as a lamb to the slaughter, and as a sheep before its shearers is dumb, so he opened not His mouth."* Just as our Lord and Savior made no resistance and did not put up a fight, neither did Joseph. God had a plan to save a nation through one man. If God had chosen you or me for that purpose, we all know the outcome would have been vastly different.

Meanwhile, back home, the brothers returned with Joseph's coat of many colors, soaked in the blood of a kid goat. When Jacob saw the coat, which held great sentimental value to him, he tore his clothes, put on sackcloth, and mourned for his son for many days, believing his beloved son was dead.

FULL CIRCLE

Everything changed in a heartbeat for Joseph. One thing was certain: Israel was behind him, and Egypt was before him. He was probably saddled on a donkey, horse, or camel, reflecting that he had no right or privilege to ride in a chariot. This journey into unknown territory marked a profound turning point in his life. In this transition, Joseph had lost his:

- Name

- Identity

- Family

- Liberty

- Culture

- Language

- Rights and privileges

Once a dreamer filled with great potential and promise, Joseph had lost everything, reduced to becoming a slave. He was to be disregarded wherever he went—no special treatment, no reserved seats, no colorful garments. Instead, he would be treated with the same contempt and disdain as all slaves.

In Genesis 42, God's plan, hidden since the foundation of the world, begins to unfold in full circle. A famine strikes Israel, and Jacob instructs his sons to go to Egypt for corn. By this time, Joseph, who had been sold into slavery years earlier, had been appointed governor, second in command to Pharaoh. It is believed that Joseph was 17 years old when he was sold into slavery, but it took 22 years for God's plan and Joseph's dreams to fully materialize.

Joseph reveals his identity to his brothers after a series of events involving corn, cups, and a scheme to bring his younger brother to Egypt. In Genesis 45:3-5, Joseph declares, "I am Joseph your brother, whom ye sold... God did send me before you to preserve life." His brothers were instantly sick to their stomachs at this jaw-dropping, breathtaking, and eye-bulging moment.

This moment of truth was as if the world had stopped revolving around its orbits. Joseph acknowledges that his journey was painful and long, but he recognizes God's hand in it all. He sees God's plan as more important than the intentions of his brothers. Though they sold him into slavery, God sent him ahead to preserve lives.

The question now is this: **Can you see God in your situation?** Look keenly, and when you find Him, you will find peace in what God is doing.

When we learn to put the past behind us—to forgive as Esau forgave Jacob, to recognize God's sovereign plan as Joseph did—we open ourselves to the healing and restoration that can only come through reconciliation. The hurts of yesterday need not define our tomorrow.

Like Joseph, we can declare, "You meant it for evil, but God meant it for good" (Genesis 50:20). This is the power of letting go, of refusing to be prisoners of past pain, and of embracing God's redemptive purpose for our lives.

Remember, forgiveness is not about forgetting what happened; it's about choosing not to let it control your future. It's about releasing the burden of bitterness and making room for God's blessing. As Scripture teaches us in Philippians 3:13-14, "Brothers, I do not consider that I have made it my own. But one thing I do: forgetting what lies behind and straining forward to what lies ahead, I press on toward the goal for the prize of the upward call of God in Christ Jesus."

Put the past behind you. God has greater things ahead.

Chapter 6

OFFENDED BY THE TRUTH

Several years ago, I worked overnight as a central supply technician at Lurie Children's Hospital in the heart of Chicago. We had built a remarkable team of young people who worked well together. The midnight crew, as we were called, included people like Deja, Berto, Nancy, Dominique, and Shalonda. Though some came and went, most of us remained.

One night, during our break, we sat down to eat. One of us had a footlong Subway sandwich and then went on to unwrap a second footlong to eat. Out of surprise, I asked, "Are you going to eat that second sandwich after finishing the first?"

One of our friends nearby interjected, "Oh my God, Ebo, you judge so much."

I replied, "I'm not judging—I'm just concerned about my friend."

This small exchange illuminates a much larger issue. In today's generation, everything is labeled as judgment, making it nearly impossible to tell someone they are doing something concerning, even when the intention comes from a place of love. There is a near-zero tolerance for truth, even when it is tempered with humility, caution, and genuine care. Sometimes, I wonder if this generation could listen to an entire sermon from Jesus without being offended.

TRUTH SPOKEN IN LOVE VS. JUDGMENT

There exists a crucial distinction between speaking truth from a place of love and passing judgment from a position of superiority. When we care about someone, we naturally become concerned about choices that might harm them—physically, emotionally, or spiritually. This concern compels us to speak up, not to condemn, but to protect and guide. However, our culture has increasingly conflated genuine concern with judgment, creating an environment where any form of loving correction is met with defensiveness.

Ephesians 4:15 encourages us to "speak the truth in love," recognizing that truth without love can be harsh and damaging, while love without truth lacks substance and direction. The midnight crew at the hospital had formed bonds of friendship that should have allowed for honest communication. Yet, even in that close-knit environment, expressing concern was misinterpreted as judgment.

THE JESUS MODEL

Jesus had a unique ability to discern the hearts of His listeners and tailor His message to meet their needs. Yet, His words often pierced deeply. For instance, in Matthew 16:23, Jesus calls Peter "Satan." Of course, He was addressing the spirit that had manipulated Peter at that moment. Still, can you imagine your reaction if your pastor called you "Satan" after a slip of the tongue or a moment of thoughtlessness?

It's worth noting that earlier in Matthew 16:16-17, Peter had received a profound revelation that Jesus was the Messiah, a truth so significant that it prompted a blessing from Jesus. He declared Peter to be the rock upon which the Church would be built. However, in the same chapter, the "rock" became a stumbling block to the Messiah.

In the very next chapter, Matthew 17, Jesus takes Peter, James, and John up a mountain, where they witness His transfiguration—a life-changing moment. Peter responds by saying, "Master, it is good for us to be here." Peter's heart was open to receiving truth and correction, a quality that is rare in our generation.

Peter was neither angry nor offended when Jesus called him Satan. He could have stormed off, declaring, "How dare you call me that!" Can you imagine the Jew being called Satan? Yet Peter recovered from the sharp rebuke. He didn't isolate himself or refuse to participate in the group's mission. Instead, he continued with his assignment and followed every instruction given to him.

THE PERFECT PICTURE

In Matthew 23:13-28, Jesus delivers a series of rebukes to the Pharisees, calling them hypocrites, vipers, and whitewashed tombs. These words deeply offended the Pharisees, who were religious leaders highly regarded for their piety, strict adherence to the law, and public image as righteous men. Jesus' accusations not only challenged their authority but also exposed the hypocrisy underlying their perceived righteousness.

The Pharisees saw themselves as spiritual leaders of Israel. They were considered experts in the Law and were highly respected by the people for their devotion and religious practices. However, when Jesus called them hypocrites (Matthew 23:13-15), He exposed their behavior as outwardly pious but inwardly corrupt. He accused them of preventing others from entering the kingdom of God while elevating themselves to positions of honor. For the Pharisees, this was a direct challenge to their authority and influence over the people.

Jesus' words undermined their status as the spiritual guides of the nation and exposed the disparity between their external actions and internal hearts. They believed they were acting in accordance with God's will, and to be labeled as hypocrites was not just an insult but an attack on their entire sense of righteousness.

WHY WE GET OFFENDED BY TRUTH

There are several reasons why people—then and now—find themselves offended by truth:

1. Truth Challenges Our Self-Image

When someone points out something that contradicts how we see ourselves, it creates cognitive dissonance. We have constructed narratives about who we are, and when truth challenges those narratives, our natural response is often defensiveness. The Pharisees prided themselves on their rigorous observance of the law. They were known for their meticulousness in keeping religious traditions and for their public displays of righteousness, such as giving to the poor, praying, and fasting.

When Jesus called them whitewashed tombs (Matthew 23:27-28), He was pointing out that, although they appeared clean and righteous on the outside, they were spiritually dead and corrupt on the inside. This was a direct critique of their self-righteousness. The Pharisees believed that their adherence to the letter of the law made them morally superior to others, but Jesus exposed the fact that their actions were often motivated by pride, arrogance, and a desire for public recognition rather than genuine love for God or others. This rejection of their self-righteousness and public persona was offensive to the Pharisees, as it contradicted everything they held dear.

2. Truth Exposes What We Hide

We all have aspects of ourselves we prefer to keep hidden—weaknesses, insecurities, or behaviors we know are problematic. When someone speaks truth that shines a light on these hidden areas, it can feel like a violation of our privacy or an attack on our character.

Jesus also referred to the Pharisees as vipers (Matthew 23:33), implying that they were deceitful and poisonous. Vipers are dangerous, not only because they strike unexpectedly but because their venom is hidden until it is too late. By using this term, Jesus accused them of leading others astray with their false teachings and misleading spiritual practices. The Pharisees had created a religious system that burdened people with heavy rules and regulations while offering no genuine path to spiritual renewal. Jesus' accusations revealed that their external religious practices were devoid of true spirituality. The Pharisees, who prided themselves on their ritual purity and piety, were spiritually blind. They were offended because Jesus was exposing their empty spiritual practices, which had no real connection to the heart of God.

3. Truth Requires Change

Perhaps the most challenging aspect of truth is that, once acknowledged, it often demands a response. When we recognize a truth about ourselves that requires change, we face the uncomfortable choice of either changing or living in denial. Sometimes, it's easier to reject the truth-teller than to embrace the difficult path of transformation.

The Pharisees were deeply concerned with appearances and public perception, going to great lengths to maintain an image of righteousness through external actions. They engaged in lengthy prayers, ostentatious acts of charity, and strict observance of rituals to project their piety. However, Jesus accused them of hypocrisy, highlighting their outward display of righteousness while inwardly being filled with pride, greed, and deceit (Matthew 23:25-26). By calling them hypocrites, Jesus exposed the gap between their public image and their private lives. The Pharisees were offended because their self-constructed image of holiness was being torn down by Jesus' words. To be called a hypocrite was not only a personal insult but also a rejection of their self-proclaimed status as spiritual authorities.

4. Truth Threatens Our Comfort

We naturally gravitate toward comfort and away from discomfort. Truth often disrupts our comfortable patterns and routines, forcing us to confront realities we'd rather ignore. This disruption can trigger a defensive response as we attempt to preserve our comfort zones.

The Pharisees firmly believed that salvation was achieved through strict adherence to the law and religious rituals. They viewed their actions and adherence to the law as the basis of their righteousness before God. However, Jesus challenged this belief, asserting that their self-righteousness was a barrier to salvation. He pointed out that their external displays of religion were meaningless if their hearts were not aligned with God's will.

His comparison of them to "whitewashed tombs" (Matthew 23:27-28) was a stark contrast to their beliefs. In Jewish tradition, tombs were considered unclean, and whitewashing them made them appear clean on the outside while remaining unclean inside. This was a powerful image that contradicted their belief that external rituals and appearances could make them right with God. This not only offended them personally but also undermined their deeply held theological convictions about salvation.

5. Truth Challenges Authority and Control

For those in positions of power or influence, truth that undermines their authority can be especially threatening. When our status, position, or control is at stake, we're more likely to reject truth that threatens these aspects of our identity.

The Pharisees were offended because Jesus directly challenged the religious system they had built, which centered on their authority, control, and status. They had constructed a religious framework that put them at the top, elevating their authority and maintaining power over the people. Jesus' condemnation of their actions was a direct attack on this system. Jesus' accusations revealed that their religious leadership was corrupt and self-serving, focused on gaining power, influence, and wealth, rather than leading people into a deeper and genuine relationship with God. To have their leadership condemned in such a forceful manner was a direct threat to their power and influence.

FINDING BALANCE: SPEAKING TRUTH WITHOUT BEING JUDGMENTAL

So how do we navigate this delicate balance between speaking truth and avoiding judgment? Here are some principles that can guide us:

1. Check Your Motives

Before speaking truth to someone, examine your heart. Are you motivated by genuine concern for their well-being, or by a desire to feel superior or to control their behavior? Truth spoken from love looks very different from truth spoken from pride.

2. Establish Relationship First

Truth is best received in the context of established trust and relationship. When someone knows you care about them, they're more likely to hear your concerns as an expression of that care rather than as judgment. Just as Jesus had established a relationship with Peter before His rebuke, we should invest in relationships that create a foundation for truth-telling.

3. Choose the Right Time and Place

The midnight break room at the hospital might not have been the ideal setting for expressing concern about a friend's eating habits. Private conversations often allow for more vulnerable and honest exchanges than public settings where the person might feel embarrassed or defensive.

4. Use "I" Statements Instead of "You" Accusations

Instead of saying, "You're eating too much," consider saying, "I'm concerned about you because I care." This approach focuses on your feelings and concerns rather than making accusations about their behavior.

5. Be Open to Dialogue, Not Monologue

True communication involves both speaking and listening. After expressing your concern, be ready to hear the other person's perspective. They may have insights or explanations you haven't considered.

6. Accept That Not All Truth Will Be Received Well

Even when we speak truth with the purest motives and in the most loving way, some people will still be offended. Jesus, who embodied perfect love and truth, faced rejection and hostility. We should not expect to be received better than He was.

CONCLUSION: THE COURAGE TO SPEAK AND HEAR TRUTH

Ultimately, the Pharisees were offended by Jesus' words because they confronted their pride, exposed their hypocrisy, and undermined their authority. Jesus condemned their prioritization of external rituals and public appearances over true inward righteousness. By condemning their self-righteousness and revealing their spiritual emptiness, Jesus threatened the very foundation of the Pharisees' identity and authority. To them, Jesus' rebukes were not only insulting but also threatening, as they exposed the hollowness of their religious system and their personal integrity.

In our current cultural climate, where truth is often sacrificed on the altar of comfort and non-confrontation, we need both the courage to speak truth in love and the humility to hear truth about ourselves. The midnight crew at Lurie Children's Hospital taught me that even among friends, speaking truth requires wisdom and sensitivity. Yet, I remain convinced that genuine friendship and authentic community require the willingness to risk offense for the sake of love.

As followers of Christ, we are called to neither judge harshly nor remain silent when truth needs to be spoken. Instead, we're invited to follow Jesus' example—speaking truth that transforms rather than condemns, and receiving truth with the humility that leads to growth. In a world increasingly offended by truth, may we be people who both speak and embrace truth with love, courage, and grace.

"Speaking the truth in love, we are to grow up in every way into him who is the head, into Christ." - Ephesians 4:15

Chapter 7
GIVE BUT CAN'T TAKE

In this chapter, we address critical and hypersensitive individuals who often act as though they know everything. They dish out advice, even when unsolicited, and scrutinize every detail of a situation or encounter, not to seek the good but to find something to critique. These individuals constantly read between the lines, frequently offering contrary opinions. While such tendencies may stem from a discerning nature, when they become habitual, they can cause serious problems in relationships. Ironically, I have observed that these individuals are often the most easily offended when receiving the very feedback, they so freely give to others.

"Why do you look at the speck of sawdust in your brother's eye and pay no attention to the plank in your own eye? How can you say to your brother, 'Let me take the speck out of your eye,' when

all the time there is a plank in your own eye? You hypocrite, first take the plank out of your own eye, and then you will see clearly to remove the speck from your brother's eye." — Matthew 7:3-5

THE PARADOX OF GIVING COUNSEL BUT REJECTING IT

As a counselor, I recently worked with a couple facing issues related to correction and communication. One partner had difficulty accepting counsel or correction, particularly when the advice was unsolicited. After asking why there was always resistance to counsel, the other partner explained their frustration, saying, "I will not listen to him unless he decides to listen to me."

This scenario plays out in many marriages, where one partner feels superior to the other or considers their spouse a problem to be fixed or a project to be completed. Such an attitude invariably creates conflict and resentment. The giving of advice becomes one-directional rather than mutual, creating an imbalance that strains the relationship.

PARTNERS, NOT PROJECTS

We must understand that in a marriage, we are teammates working to build one another up. Counsel should stem from love, not critique. Some people are naturally defensive, while others become defensive because they feel constantly attacked. Until that perceived threat is alleviated, receiving counsel becomes difficult.

In some cases, people choose to withhold their thoughts entirely to avoid offending anyone. However, open communication is essential for healthy relationships. Partners must support each other through challenges and weaknesses, fostering growth and strength in those areas.

Defensiveness can arise from several factors, including pride, ego, and a sense of superiority. If you're dealing with any such situation, here are several recommendations that can help transform the dynamic:

PRACTICAL STEPS FOR BREAKING THROUGH DEFENSIVENESS

1. Pray

Pray for the person, and if possible, pray together. Prayer invites God's wisdom and peace into the situation, fostering understanding and unity. When we seek divine guidance, we often receive insights that help us approach difficult conversations with greater compassion and clarity.

2. Do Everything Out of Love

When people feel genuinely loved and cared for, their defenses often crumble, making them more receptive to your actions or words. While many act out of a sense of responsibility, this approach can lead to burnout. Love, however, is inexhaustible.

I always tell my wife, "Don't do anything for me out of responsibility. If you can't do it out of love, don't." This principle transforms the nature of our interactions, ensuring they're rooted in genuine care rather than obligation.

3. Ask God for Wisdom

Seek God's guidance in discerning what to communicate and how to express truth with love. Consider these principles for effective communication:

- Not every situation requires a comment.

- Learn to ignore trivial matters.

- Focus on self-improvement as much as you want to correct others.

- Talking is not the same as effective communication.

- Choose your words carefully.

- Avoid starting conversations with phrases like, "I need to talk to you" or "There's something I want to discuss." Such phrases often put people on the defensive before the conversation even begins.

4. Choose the Right Time to Talk

Timing is everything. You don't need to address issues the moment they arise. Waiting for the right time allows for a more productive and meaningful conversation. Consider the environment: is there anyone who can overhear your conversation or witness a change in attitude or mood?

What's the present mood or temperament of the person you want to talk to? For instance, if you're having a great time or your partner just had a good time with friends and family, that is not the right time to have a serious conversation. The best moments for meaningful correction often come during periods of calm and connection, not in the heat of conflict or during celebrations.

THE TRUE GOALS OF CORRECTION

1. Restoration and Growth

Always remember that the goal of correction is to build up and restore the relationship, not to alienate the other person (1 Corinthians 9:19–23). Correction should never be about proving yourself right or the other person wrong. Instead, it should aim to strengthen the bond between you and foster mutual growth.

2. Self-Awareness and Humility

Be mindful of your weaknesses and imperfections, this is a sign of humility. Such self-awareness helps you recognize potential blind spots and provides a better perspective on how others may be feeling. It also offers insight into what you need to communicate to help strengthen someone else, especially if you're familiar with the struggles they are facing.

Scripture emphasizes that not everyone is qualified to correct others. Attempting to correct someone without proper knowledge, wisdom, and understanding can often cause more harm than good. Correction requires a spiritually mature person who is mindful of their frailties and approaches the situation with humility and care.

3. The Balance of Giving and Receiving

The ultimate irony of those who "give but can't take" is that they miss out on the very growth they claim to want for others. When we close ourselves off to correction, we limit our potential and stunt our spiritual and emotional development.

Galatians 6:1-2 reminds us: *"Brothers and sisters, if someone is caught in a sin, you who live by the Spirit should restore that person gently. But watch yourselves, or you also may be tempted. Carry each other's burdens, and in this way you will fulfill the law of Christ."*

This scripture emphasizes both the importance of correction and the humility with which it should be offered. When we recognize our own susceptibility to temptation and failure, we approach others with gentleness rather than judgment.

CREATING A CULTURE OF MUTUAL GROWTH

In healthy relationships, both parties recognize their need for growth and welcome input from each other. Here are some practical ways to foster this dynamic:

1. **Regularly invite feedback**: Create opportunities for your partner to share observations about your behavior in a non-threatening context.

2. **Express gratitude for correction**: When someone points out an area where you could improve, thank them for caring enough to speak up.

3. **Lead by example**: Demonstrate how to receive correction graciously, and others may follow your lead.

4. **Celebrate growth together**: Acknowledge and appreciate the positive changes you see in each other because of mutual correction.

5. **Remember the goal**: Keep the focus on becoming more like Christ together, rather than "fixing" each other.

CONCLUSION

The ability to both give and receive correction with grace is a mark of spiritual maturity. Those who can dish out advice but cannot take it reveal a heart that is still striving for control rather than surrender. As we grow in Christ, we learn to hold our opinions loosely and our hearts open to the refining work of the Holy Spirit—often working through the honest words of those who love us.

Remember, the goal is not to be right but to be righteous—and righteousness comes through humility, love, and a willingness to be shaped by God's truth, regardless of the vessel through which it comes. When we create relationships where correction flows both ways, guided by love and received with gratitude, we create the conditions for authentic growth and lasting intimacy.

Chapter 8

FULL OF IT – DENYING SELF AND FOLLOWING CHRIST

· ⟫⟫⟫⟫⟫ ● ⟪⟪⟪⟪⟪ ·

To follow Christ fully, we must deny ourselves, take up our cross, and follow Him. This sacred surrender transcends mere suppression of desires; it demands an active process of mortifying the flesh—putting to death anything that opposes God's divine will in our lives. Through the indwelling power of the Holy Spirit, this transformation becomes not only possible, but inevitable. As we nourish our spirit through immersion in the Word, fervent prayer, purposeful fasting, and life-giving godly influences, we grow ever stronger in our relationship with the Almighty. The ultimate trajectory of our lives hinges on one crucial battle: whether our flesh or spirit dominates. When we tenderly nurture the spirit, we unlock the door to the abundant life Jesus promised—a life overflowing with purpose, peace, and divine presence.

Jesus declared with unmistakable clarity, "If any man will come after me, let him deny himself, and take up his cross, and follow me" (Matthew 16:24). These words capture the very essence of Christian discipleship: the sacred call to deny oneself to fully follow Christ. Jesus stands not as a dictator imposing His will upon us, but as a loving Savior extending an invitation that demands a response. Our capacity to embrace God's calling completely depends on our willingness to deny ourselves—to place His desires above our own.

THE GREATEST BARRIER

Selfishness forms the most formidable obstacle to cultivating an intimate relationship with God. When we elevate our needs and desires above others, we not only stifle our spiritual growth but inflict lasting damage on our relationships. This self-centeredness inevitably leads to fractured connections as we pursue our insatiable desires, often at the expense of those we claim to love.

When we lavish attention on our fleshly desires while neglecting spiritual nourishment, we exist in a state dominated by self. The flesh becomes our master, leaving our spirit withered and weak. Paul's words in Galatians 6:8 pierce through our comfortable deceptions: "For whoever sows to the flesh will of the flesh reap corruption; but whoever sows to the Spirit will of the Spirit reap everlasting life." This divine principle reveals an unshakable truth: the realm where we invest our energy determines the harvest of our lives. If we invest in the flesh, indulging in self-centered behaviors, we reap the bitter fruit of corruption. However, when we invest in the Spirit, we harvest eternal life and the profound joy of intimacy with God.

THE DANGERS OF LIVING ACCORDING TO THE FLESH

Living according to the flesh carries devastating consequences. The flesh, by its very nature, craves immediate gratification, often blind to the needs and well-being of others. We become consumed by our ego, pride, and sense of self-importance, developing a callous disregard for others' perspectives. This self-absorption renders us incapable of acknowledging mistakes, admitting shortcomings, or accepting responsibility for our actions. Instead, we point accusing fingers outward, assigning blame while evading accountability.

This inability to engage in honest self-reflection creates tension in relationships and shapes us into souls either perpetually defensive or prone to explosive emotional outbursts. If we persist in neglecting spiritual growth while fixating solely on fleshly desires, we forfeit the abundant life Jesus promises. With love and urgency, He calls us first to deny ourselves before truly following Him. This means fixing our gaze unwaveringly upon Him and striving to mortify the flesh—crucifying the sinful nature that fights for dominance. We must empty ourselves completely of sin, pride, ego, hatred, and every toxin that stands in opposition to God's perfect will.

MORTIFYING THE FLESH

Romans 8:13 declares with solemn power, "For if you live according to the flesh, you will die; but if by the Spirit you put to death the deeds of the body, you will live." The conquest of the flesh never comes through human willpower alone but through surrender to the Holy Spirit's might. The word "mortify" means to subdue or put to death—in this context, it speaks of subjugating the flesh's desires through disciplined self-denial. The flesh cannot conquer itself; only the Spirit possesses the power to overcome it. To mortify the flesh, we must depend wholly on the Holy Spirit's strength and guidance.

The flesh and spirit exist in perpetual conflict, their desires fundamentally opposed. The dominant force—whether flesh or spirit—determines the direction of our lives. If the flesh rules, it corrupts our decisions, actions, and relationships. Conversely, when we nurture the Spirit, divine wisdom guides our choices and aligns us with God's perfect will.

HOW TO STARVE THE FLESH AND FEED THE SPIRIT

Mortifying the flesh requires intentional starvation— cutting off the supply lines that empower fleshly desires. The more we feed the flesh, the stronger its grip becomes, pulling us further from God's presence. Conversely, feeding the Spirit fortifies our inner spiritual life and empowers resistance against carnal temptations.

Here are transformative practices to starve the flesh and nourish the Spirit:

The Word of God provides essential nourishment for our spirit. Through devoted reading, diligent study, and deep meditation on Scripture, we strengthen our spiritual life and gain profound insight into God's will. Jesus affirmed this truth, declaring, "Man shall not live by bread alone, but by every word that proceeds from the mouth of God" (Matthew 4:4). When we feast on God's Word, our spirit grows robust while our flesh weakens. Moreover, prayer establishes vital communion with God. In those sacred moments of connection, our hearts align with His perfect will, and

His presence permeates our being. Consistent, fervent prayer cultivates spiritual vitality and supplies divine strength to resist temptation's pull. Through prayer, we acknowledge our dependence on God and invite His transforming power into every aspect of our lives.

Fasting likewise represents a profound act of self-denial. By willingly abstaining from food or other desires, we demonstrate our complete dependence on God and submission to His will. This spiritual discipline breaks the flesh's dominion and heightens our sensitivity to the Spirit's gentle promptings. Furthermore, in our digital age, we must vigilantly monitor what we consume. Ungodly social media content, secular music glorifying worldly values, and entertainment that celebrates sin all nourish the flesh's appetites. To feed the Spirit, we must choose our influences wisely, ensuring they align with Kingdom values and nurture spiritual growth rather than fleshly desires.

Finally, relationships profoundly impact our spiritual journey. Surrounding ourselves with those who encourage godliness and provide loving accountability proves essential for spiritual flourishing. Toxic or ungodly relationships can undermine spiritual progress and feed fleshly tendencies. As Scripture warns, "Bad company corrupts good character" (1 Corinthians 15:33). The community we choose either propels us toward Christ or pulls us toward the world.

When we commit to denying self—mortifying the flesh and feeding the spirit—we position ourselves to experience the fullness of life in Christ. This journey demands daily surrender, constant vigilance, and complete dependence on the Holy Spirit. Yet the rewards far outweigh the sacrifice: intimate fellowship with God, freedom from sin's bondage, and the joy of reflecting Christ to a broken world. As we die to self, we truly begin to live.

Chapter 9

FAMILIARITY

There is a subtle yet devastating trap that many fall into—not through rebellion or malice, but through unchecked proximity. It doesn't shout; it whispers. It doesn't strike suddenly; it corrodes overtime. This trap is *familiarity*.

We often speak of betrayal, pride, or jealousy as the great saboteurs of relationships, but familiarity may be the most deceptive of them all. It masquerades as closeness. It wears the face of comfort. It thrives in proximity and shared history, and if we are not vigilant, it slowly strips away honor, erodes respect, and replaces awe with apathy. What once inspired us begins to irritate us. What once impressed us now feels common. The sacred becomes ordinary. The anointed becomes "just another person."

The old saying, *"Familiarity breeds contempt,"* holds a timeless truth. While closeness should deepen love and trust, when left unguarded, it often does the opposite, it opens the door to criticism, contempt, and ultimately, offense. In our marriages, ministries, families, and friendships, many wounds are not caused by strangers, but by those who know us best.

THE OFFENSE OF THE FAMILIAR: MIRIAM AND AARON

Nowhere is this more evident than in the story of Moses, his sister Miriam, and his brother Aaron:

"Miriam and Aaron spoke against Moses because of the Cushite woman whom he had married... They said, "Has the Lord indeed spoken only through Moses?" Has He not spoken through us also?' And the Lord heard it... The Lord said, 'With him I speak face to face... Why then were you not afraid to speak against My servant Moses?"' — Numbers 12:1–8

Consider the context. Miriam and Aaron weren't outsiders; they were family. They had walked with Moses, served with him, seen his flaws, and perhaps reminded him of them often. They likely remembered his past, his failures, his fears, his stutter. But they had forgotten one thing: *God chose him.*

Familiarity blinded them to Moses' divine assignment. They were offended by his marriage, but the deeper issue was their struggle to accept that someone they had helped raise, someone they thought they understood, could carry such a unique weight of glory. And so, their speech drifted into dishonor. Their offense wasn't just against Moses—it was against God's decision.

Let this sink in: **they saw a brother, but God saw a servant.** And when they dishonored Moses, they dishonored the One who called him. God's response was clear and terrifying—He came down in a cloud and said, in essence, *"This man may be your brother, but he is My prophet. Why were you not afraid?"*

In our own lives, how often do we diminish those closest to us simply because we know too much? We've seen their process, so we question their position. We've seen their past, so we doubt their promotion. But God's perspective is not limited by history—He sees calling, not comfort. And He expects us to honor those He has chosen, even if we've known them since childhood.

FAMILIARITY WITH JESUS: A PROPHET WITHOUT HONOR

This same tension reappeared centuries later in the ministry of Jesus:

"Where did this man get this wisdom and these mighty works? Is not this the carpenter's son?... And they took offense at him. But Jesus said to them, 'A prophet is not without honor except in his hometown and in his own household.'" — Matthew 13:54–57

The Messiah Himself was rejected by the people who should have celebrated Him the most. They were not angry about His miracles; they were offended by His origin. They stumbled not over His teaching, but over His familiarity. They thought they knew who He was: "Isn't this Joseph's son?" In their eyes, He had no right to be more than what they remembered.

This is what familiarity does. It shrinks people down to the limits of our past experience with them. We create a ceiling for others based on what we've seen, rather than what God is doing. We reject their growth, their transformation, and their calling because we think we *already know* who they are.

Jesus didn't rebuke them for questioning. He mourned the missed opportunity. *"A prophet is not without honor..."* His power wasn't diminished, but their access to it was.

96

Dishonor limits what we can receive from those God sends. Offense doesn't weaken the anointed—it blocks us from the blessing they carry.

HOW FAMILIARITY BREEDS OFFENSE TODAY

Offense born out of familiarity is rampant today—in marriages, ministries, teams, and families. A wife compares her husband's shortcomings to another man's strengths. A church member resents their pastor's imperfections while idolizing voices they hear online. A leader dismisses faithful team members simply because they've become too familiar.

Familiarity clouds judgment. It makes us forget that every person—no matter how close—is still a work of God's grace. The longer we walk with someone, the more intentional we must be to honor the call of God on their life. Honor must be discipline, not just an emotion. It must be rooted in reverence for God, not preference for personalities.

And yet, the responsibility goes both ways.

Leaders, don't despise questions from those close to you. Sometimes offense is borne not in rebellion but in a lack of clarity. When questioned, don't be defensive. Instead, use the opportunity to:

- **Clarify** – Not all questions are attacks; many are born from confusion.

- **Inform** – Don't assume people understand your decisions; tell the story behind them.

- **Educate** – Give people tools to grow in understanding.

- **Impact** – Show grace. You lead better when you teach through tension.

Jesus, even when rejected, did not retaliate. He continued in purpose, driven by divine identity, not human validation.

OVERCOMING THE OFFENSE OF THE FAMILIAR

If you find yourself on the receiving end of offense—misunderstood by those closest to you—do not let bitterness grow. Their rejection does not define your value. Christ, too, was rejected by His own, yet He did not abandon His mission. Use rejection as refining fire. Let it kill your need for approval and deepen your dependency on God.

"He was despised and rejected by men... a man of sorrows and acquainted with grief... but He was pierced for our transgressions..." — Isaiah 53:3–5

If you've allowed familiarity to cloud your vision of someone, repent. Ask God to restore your honor for them. Pray for fresh eyes to see their divine assignment. Remember: what's familiar to you is still sacred to God.

In every relationship, whether close or distant— choose reverence over routine, and honor over offense. Familiarity is not the enemy, but without humility, it will become one.

Chapter 10

MY RIGHT

As a citizen of any nation, there are certain rights we enjoy—some by birth, others conferred through naturalization or acquired in other ways. Rights flow to us by reason of what we do, what position we occupy, or how much service we have rendered over the years. Regardless of their origin, being stripped of these rights strikes at the very core of our identity, becoming a profound source of offense for virtually every soul who walks this earth. At some juncture in our journey, we have all felt the sting of violation when our rights were denied or trampled upon. These rights—whether bestowed or earned—become sacred territory within our hearts, and we would move mountains to preserve them.

Yet here lies one of life's great paradoxes: with magnificent rights comes sobering responsibility. The very rights we clutch so tightly should never become weapons that wound others, nor should they transform us into beings perpetually primed for offense. Wisdom demands we develop a keen awareness of the circumstances that trigger indignation and cultivate the spiritual muscle to resist our natural inclination toward being offended. Simultaneously, we must navigate this world with the delicate grace required to exercise our rights without crushing the rights of those around us.

The streets of Chicago offer a daily theater where this human drama unfolds before my eyes. The urban landscape pulses with humanity—rivers of people with headphones creating personal sanctuaries amid the chaos, commuters clutching coffee cups like lifelines, elevated trains thundering overhead like metallic dragons, and drivers punctuating the symphony with impatient horns. But nothing captures the essence of our relationship with rights quite like watching pedestrians stride confidently into traffic simply because the law grants them passage. Some cross with eyes locked on approaching drivers, their expressions a silent challenge: *I dare you to violate my right of way.*

I often find myself pondering the curious calculus behind such boldness. Would they truly sacrifice limb or life upon the altar of being right? Many don't even perform the basic survival ritual of looking both ways, so complete is their faith in their protected status. This behavior illuminates the extraordinary value we place on our rights—a value so immense that rational self-preservation sometimes takes a back seat to their exercise. The speed with which we detect and decry any infringement upon our rights reveals how deeply they're intertwined with our sense of justice and worth.

One crisp autumn morning, while navigating the school drop-off gauntlet with my children, we approached a four-way stop near their elementary school. Another parent, clearly racing against the merciless school bell, abruptly cut into our lane, claiming the right of way that rightfully belonged to us. My children—ages seven, five, and four—erupted with a moral outrage that both amused and startled me. "Daddy, that driver cut us off! We had the right of way!" Their indignation burned white-hot, their sense of justice inflamed. Testing their conviction, I asked simply, "Are you sure?" They responded with the unshakable certainty that only children possess, their voices forming a unified chorus: "Yes!"

Attempting to model a different approach, I offered calmly, "That's okay. Perhaps they're in a hurry." But my children would not be so easily pacified in the face of such a clear moral breach. They shot back with the moral absolutism of youth: "It's never okay to cut!" In that moment, I realized how early the seeds of fairness take root in human consciousness—waiting your turn, standing in line, respecting the invisible boundaries that maintain social order. These seemingly small lessons about rights and fairness carry the power to ignite our deepest emotions, revealing how fundamentally they shape our understanding of justice.

Against this backdrop of human nature's fierce attachment to rights, let us turn our gaze to how Jesus— the embodiment of divine wisdom—navigated these same waters:

"And when they had come to Capernaum, they that received tribute money came to Peter and said, 'Doth not your master pay tribute?' He saith, 'Yes,' and when he was come into the house, Jesus prevented him, saying, 'What thinkest thou, Simon? Of whom do the kings of the earth take custom or tribute? Of their own children, or of strangers?' Peter saith unto him, 'Of strangers.' Jesus saith unto him, 'Then are the children free?'" (Matthew 17:24-26)

"Notwithstanding, lest we should offend them, go thou to the sea and cast a hook and take up the fish that first cometh up; and when thou hast opened his mouth thou shalt find a piece of money: that take and give unto them for me and thee." (Matthew 17:27)

Here stands Jesus—the Lord of the temple itself— agreeing to pay taxes for that very temple. By every conceivable right, He stood exempt. The temple tax was required of every Jewish man, yet Jesus illuminated the deeper truth to Peter: If I am the Lord of the temple, this tax that supports My mission and furthers My divine agenda should not apply to Me. Despite this irrefutable logic, Jesus chose a path that defies our natural instincts—He refused to insist on His right to exemption. Instead, He uttered words that should shake the foundations of our rights-obsessed culture: "Let's pay the tax to avoid causing offense."

Even more remarkably, knowing they lacked the funds for this obligation, Jesus was prepared to manifest a miracle rather than allow priests, citizens, church members, or Pharisees to stumble over His exercise of rightful exemption. This supernatural provision not only resolved the immediate financial dilemma but strengthened Peter's faith and conveyed a masterclass in respecting authority, even when one stands above it.

Here emerges the profound insight that might transform our approach to rights entirely: Jesus laid down His life for humanity, but it's crucial to recognize that He first laid down His rights. This passage reveals Jesus' extraordinary humility and voluntary submission to earthly laws and customs, despite His divine prerogative to transcend them. It showcases His exquisite sensitivity to avoiding unnecessary offense or creating obstacles for others in their religious practice.

The surrender of our rights often demands genuine sacrifice and concerted effort, but the dividends—peace that passes understanding, unity among the divided, and relationships fortified against the storms of life—represent a treasure beyond calculation.

LESSONS FROM JESUS' HANDLING OF RIGHTS

1. Humility and Willingness to Submit

Though Jesus existed as the very Son of God, exempt from the constraints that bind mere mortals, He demonstrated breathtaking humility by voluntarily placing Himself under those same constraints. He declined to assert His divine rights, choosing instead the path of peace over conflict. Philippians 2:6-8 captures this astonishing reality: Jesus, "though in the form of God, did not count equality with God a thing to be grasped, but emptied Himself, taking the form of a servant." Here we witness divinity choosing submission when assertion was fully justified.

2. Avoiding Offense

Jesus consistently prioritized relationships over rights, avoiding unnecessary offense that might create barriers between souls. While Jesus could have rightfully declared His exemption from the temple tax as the Son of God, He chose the path of accommodation rather than assertion. The Apostle Paul would later echo this Christ-like approach in 1 Corinthians 8:9, urging believers to ensure that "this liberty of yours does not somehow become a stumbling block to the weak." This principle reveals that the exercise of rights, however legitimate, must always be tempered by love.

3. Fulfilling the Law

Jesus did not arrive to demolish the law but to fulfill it completely (Matthew 5:17). His payment of the tax demonstrated profound respect for Jewish customs and earthly authorities, revealing His commitment to honoring established practices as a central element of God's redemptive mission. This teaches us that submission to legitimate authority often forms part of our spiritual calling, even when exemption might be justified.

4. Sovereignty Over Creation

In this remarkable narrative, Jesus displays His absolute sovereignty over creation by directing Peter to catch a fish containing precisely the coin needed for their tax obligation. This miraculous provision demonstrates Jesus' divine authority over the natural world and His ability to meet needs through extraordinary means. While possessing every right to refuse payment,

Jesus chose instead to fulfill the obligation through supernatural intervention—not from necessity, but to prevent unnecessary disturbance or offense. This reveals that true power often manifests not in demanding one's rights but in finding creative solutions that maintain harmony.

5. A Teaching Opportunity

Jesus transformed this potentially contentious moment into an eternal teaching for Peter—and by extension, all who would follow Him across the centuries. Through their conversation, He established His rightful exemption as the Son of God yet immediately chose not to exercise that legitimate right. This action crystallized the revolutionary values of humility, submission to authority, and the supreme importance of maintaining peace.

Through this single interaction, Jesus taught that preserving relationships and harmony frequently outweighs the satisfaction of asserting even our most legitimate rights. His example calls His followers to evaluate the greater good beyond personal vindication, adopting an attitude of selflessness and grace that transcends the natural human impulse to demand what is rightfully ours.

In a world increasingly defined by the aggressive assertion of rights, this counter-cultural wisdom offers a revolutionary alternative—choosing connection over correctness, peace over privilege, and love over legality. It invites us to transform ordinary moments of potential conflict into extraordinary demonstrations of grace that reflect the character of Christ Himself. Perhaps no spiritual discipline tests our maturity more profoundly than our willingness to occasionally lay down our rights for the sake of something greater.

What rights might you need to surrender today? What legitimate privileges could you set aside to preserve the fragile fabric of relationships in your life? Though the cost may seem steep in the moment, the treasures of peace, unity, and strengthened bonds that result from such sacrifice constitute riches that neither moth nor rust can destroy.

Chapter 11

PURSUE PEACE

⟶≫≫≫≫≫⟩ • ⟨≪≪≪≪≪≪⟵

"Let us therefore follow after the things which make for peace and things wherewith one may edify another." — Romans 14:19

THE SACRED PURSUIT

To "follow after" implies an intentional, deliberate pursuit. We are called to identify and actively chase after those elements that foster peace, not waiting passively for harmony to manifest in our lives. Peace requires our diligent pursuit of unity, forgiveness, reconciliation, and harmony. This pursuit must be active and unwavering if we truly desire peace to reign in our hearts and relationships.

Consider this profound truth: we cannot fully experience the blessing of relationships—whether in our homes, workplaces, or communities—if peace is absent. We must pursue peace to such an extent that the presence of difficult individuals no longer disturbs our inner tranquility, no matter how challenging their behavior may be.

Christ himself proclaimed, "Blessed are the peacemakers: for they shall be called the children of God" (Matthew 5:9). Being a peacemaker is not merely a commendable quality—it is a distinguishing mark of every child of God. Just as our Heavenly Father reconciled with sinners to establish peace, we too must become initiators of peace and embrace the calling to live harmoniously with everyone.

Moreover, we are divinely positioned to mediate peace between those at odds with one another. This sacred responsibility requires wisdom, knowledge, and temperance—spiritual qualities that the Holy Spirit cultivates within us as we walk in obedience.

LIVING OUT ROMANS 14:19

"Let us therefore make every effort to do what leads to peace and to mutual edification." —Romans 14:19

In a world fractured by division and conflict, the Apostle Paul's exhortation offers both a challenge and a beacon for believers seeking to embody their faith authentically. This scripture calls us to actively pursue two interconnected goals: peace and mutual edification. The deliberate phrase "make every effort" reveals that pursuing peace is not a passive stance but requires intentional, persistent action.

THE PROFOUND NATURE OF BIBLICAL PEACE

The peace Paul references transcends the mere absence of conflict. In biblical understanding, peace—"shalom" in Hebrew—encompasses wholeness, completeness, and right relationships with God, others, and within us. This peace is simultaneously a divine gift and a responsibility we are called to actively cultivate in every dimension of our lives.

When Paul instructs us to "do what leads to peace," he urges believers to:

- Carefully consider how our words and actions impact others

- Elevate unity above personal preferences and desires

- Seek deep understanding before forming judgments

- Practice radical forgiveness and genuine reconciliation

113

- Set aside non-essential differences for the sake of greater harmony

THE DIVINE CONNECTION TO MUTUAL EDIFICATION

Paul brilliantly pairs the pursuit of peace with mutual edification, the intentional building up of one another. This profound connection reveals that authentic peace isn't merely avoiding conflict but actively contributing to others' spiritual growth and well-being. When we pursue peace, we create a fertile environment where people can flourish and mature in their faith journey.

PRACTICAL PATHWAYS TO PEACE

1. Begin with Earnest Prayer

Cultivating peace begins with our relationship with God, the ultimate source of all peace. Regular, fervent prayer aligns our hearts with His purposes and grants us divine wisdom for navigating complex relationships. As we commune with the Prince of Peace, His nature increasingly becomes our own.

2. Master the Art of Active Listening

Take sacred time to genuinely understand others' perspectives, especially amid disagreement. Listening not simply to formulate a response but to truly comprehend the heart behind the words builds the foundation for peaceful relationships. Remember that God gave us two ears and one mouth—perhaps a divine hint about their proportional use.

3. Choose Words That Heal and Unite

Words possess extraordinary power to either construct peace or create discord. Speaking with grace, truth, and kindness fosters an atmosphere where peace can flourish. As Proverbs 16:24 reminds us, "Pleasant words are as a honeycomb, sweet to the soul, and health to the bones."

4. Pursue Reconciliation Relentlessly

When conflicts inevitably arise, take the initiative to restore relationships with courage and humility. This may require difficult conversations, heartfelt apologies, or extending forgiveness when it seems impossible. Our Lord modeled this by pursuing reconciliation with us even when we were still His enemies.

5. Focus on Our Common Heritage in Christ

While differences are inevitable in human relationships, focusing on what unites us—particularly our shared faith in Christ—helps maintain peace within the body of believers. We share one Lord, one faith, one baptism, one God and Father of all (Ephesians 4:5-6).

OUR SACRED RESPONSIBILITY

"If it is possible, as much as depends on you, live peaceably with all men." — Romans 12:18

Scripture assigns us personal responsibility for fostering peace. Paul's phrase "if it is possible" acknowledges that peace may not always be attainable, but it often is when pursued with godly determination. His encouragement that "as much as depends on you" places the obligation squarely on our shoulders—we must never be the reason peace disintegrates; rather, we should exhaust every option within our power to ensure peace prevails.

Achieving this divine standard often demands cooperation and sacrifice. At times, our faith may require difficult and uncomfortable actions that worldly wisdom might label as foolish. Yet such sacrificial choices reflect the love that flows from a humble, surrendered heart and serve as powerful evidence of true self-denial, following in the footsteps of our Lord.

THE HIGHER STANDARD OF CHRIST

In His transformative Sermon on the Mount, Jesus elevated our understanding of peace:

"You have heard that it was said, 'An eye for an eye and a tooth for a tooth.' But I tell you not to resist an evil person. But whoever slaps you on your right cheek, turn the other to him also. If anyone wants to sue you and take away your tunic, let him have your cloak also. And whoever compels you to go one mile, go with him two. Give to him who asks you, and from him who wants to borrow from you do not turn away." — Matthew 5:38-42

From this revolutionary teaching, we must conclude:

- We must never seek retribution or revenge

- Violence is never the solution to conflict

- The path of peace requires going beyond minimum requirements

- Grace and compassion must characterize our every response

THE PATHWAY TO RECONCILIATION

"Moreover, if your brother sins against you, go and tell him about his fault between you and him alone. If he hears you, you have gained your brother. But if he will not hear, take with you one or two more, that 'by the mouth of two or three witnesses every word may be established.' And if he refuses to hear them, tell the church. But if he refuses even to hear the church, let him be to you like a heathen and a tax collector." — Matthew 18:15-17

This passage outlines the divine process for pursuing reconciliation when offended. These are not mere suggestions but sacred instructions that should be deeply embedded in our hearts. Yet how rarely do we practice these steps! For many believers, these words lie dormant in our spiritual archives, honored in theory but neglected in practice.

May the Holy Spirit breathe new life into this teaching, empowering us to pursue peace with the same passion and persistence with which Christ pursued us. As we do, we become living testimonies to a watching world that desperately needs to witness the transformative power of biblical peace.

Let us therefore commit ourselves anew to this noble calling—making every effort to pursue peace and build one another up for God's glory and the advancement of His kingdom. For in doing so, we not only experience the blessing of peace ourselves but become channels through which God's peace flows to a broken and divided world.

Chapter 12

ETERNAL DEBTORS

In the economy of divine grace, we encounter a profound paradox: while God's love and forgiveness flow freely to humanity despite our transgressions, our obligation to forgive becomes the singular condition that can impede this divine mercy. This principle, fundamental to Christian theology, merits careful examination.

The immutable nature of God establishes the paradigm for forgiveness. His character, consistent and unchanging, demonstrates impartial benevolence— bestowing blessings indiscriminately upon the righteous and the unrighteous. This divine magnanimity extends to all aspects of His interaction with humanity, with one crucial exception: the reciprocal requirement of forgiveness. As explicitly stated in Mark 11:26:

*"But if you do not forgive, neither will
your Father which is in heaven forgive your
trespasses."*

HUMANITY AS ETERNAL DEBTORS

At the heart of this theological framework lies a radical
truth: we exist as eternal debtors in the economy of
divine grace. Our debt to God—accrued through
innumerable transgressions against infinite holiness—
remains fundamentally unpayable through our own
merit or effort. This state of perpetual indebtedness
defines our spiritual condition.

The acknowledgment of this eternal debt forms the
foundation of genuine spiritual humility. We stand
before God not as occasional transgressors who have
momentarily fallen short, but as constitutional debtors
whose very nature places us in a position of perpetual
need for mercy. As the Apostle Paul laments in Romans
7:24, "Wretched man that I am! Who will deliver me
from this body of death?"

Our status as eternal debtors manifests in several
dimensions:

1. **Moral Indebtedness:** Each transgression of divine
   law compounds our moral debt beyond calculation.

2. **Existential Indebtedness:** Our very existence and sustenance depend on God's continuous grace.

3. **Relational Indebtedness:** Our capacity to love and be loved flows from prior divine love lavished upon us.

This comprehensive indebtedness establishes the context for all discussions of forgiveness. We do not forgive others from a position of moral superiority or magnanimous charity, but from the humbling recognition of our own far greater forgiven debt.

THE CONDITIONAL NATURE OF DIVINE FORGIVENESS

The scriptural mandate regarding forgiveness represents the sole instance where divine forgiveness becomes contingent upon human action. When we withhold forgiveness from others, we effectively establish a barrier to receiving God's forgiveness ourselves. This principle operates as a divine checkpoint, where God's normally unrestricted grace encounters a deliberate limitation.

This conditionality takes on profound significance when viewed through the lens of eternal indebtedness. As perpetual recipients of divine clemency, our refusal to extend forgiveness to fellow debtors represents a fundamental misunderstanding of our position.

It betrays a spiritual amnesia—a forgetting of the astronomical debt from which we ourselves have been released.

The paradox intensifies when we consider that God's nature is boundless love, yet He institutes this singular boundary. The requirement to forgive serves not as divine pettiness but as a mechanism to align our hearts with His. Our willingness to forgive becomes the litmus test of whether we have truly understood and internalized the mercy we ourselves seek.

THE PARABLE OF UNEQUAL DEBTS

Matthew 18:23–33 presents a compelling illustration of this principle through the parable of the unmerciful servant. This narrative contrasts two debts:

- **The Greater Debt**: A servant owing his king the equivalent of ten thousand talents—an astronomical sum representing multiple lifetimes of wages.

- **The Lesser Debt**: A fellow servant owing the first servant one hundred denarii—roughly equivalent to three months' wages.

The mathematical disproportion is staggering—the first debt exceeds the second by a factor of hundreds of thousands. This deliberate hyperbole underscores the vast difference between our offenses against God and the comparatively minor infractions committed against us.

This parable serves as the most explicit biblical illustration of our status as eternal debtors. The ten thousand talents represent an amount deliberately chosen to be unpayable—a sum so vast that the servant could labor for multiple lifetimes without hope of satisfying it. This impossible debt mirrors our position before God—possessing obligations we cannot fulfill through our own resources.

The parable's progression reveals several critical insights:

1. **Initial Mercy**: The king, moved by compassion, forgives an insurmountable debt that could never realistically be repaid.

2. **Failed Response**: The pardoned servant, rather than emulating this mercy, demands immediate repayment of a comparatively insignificant sum.

3. **Ultimate Consequence**: The king revokes his forgiveness upon learning of the servant's failure to extend mercy to others.

The forgiven servant's fundamental error was forgetting his identity as a debtor. Having received extraordinary clemency, he immediately reverted to thinking of himself as a creditor with legitimate claims. This cognitive dissonance—this inability to maintain awareness of his primary identity as a forgiven debtor—led to his downfall.

The narrative concludes with the sobering pronouncement that our heavenly Father will likewise deal with those who refuse to forgive "from the heart." The addition of this phrase—"from the heart"— suggests that perfunctory or superficial forgiveness falls short of the divine requirement. True forgiveness must emanate from our innermost being.

THE PERPETUAL CYCLE OF GRACE

The recognition of our status as eternal debtors initiates what might be called the perpetual cycle of grace. Having received incalculable mercy, we become conduits of that same mercy to others. Our forgiveness of comparatively minor offenses completes the circuit, allowing divine grace to flow unimpeded both to and through us.

This cycle reflects the proper functioning of the divine economy, where grace received becomes grace extended. The eternal debtor, properly understanding their position, becomes paradoxically wealthy in the currency of forgiveness—able to dispense freely what they have freely received.

The alternative—breaking this cycle by withholding forgiveness—creates a spiritual short circuit. The eternal debtor who refuses to forgive effectively declares bankruptcy in the economy of grace, forfeiting access to resources they desperately need. As Jesus warned in the conclusion to the parable, such a one will be "delivered to the tormentors"—not as arbitrary punishment, but as the natural consequence of severing oneself from the flow of divine mercy.

THE PSYCHOLOGICAL DIMENSIONS OF FORGIVENESS

Beyond its theological significance, forgiveness carries profound psychological implications. Modern research increasingly confirms what scripture has long maintained: harboring unforgiveness creates a prison for the one who refuses to forgive, not for the offender. Resentment becomes a corrosive force, gradually consuming the vessel that contains it.

The recognition of our status as eternal debtors provides psychological liberation. When we embrace this identity, we release the burden of maintaining moral superiority. We no longer expend emotional energy cataloging others' offenses against us, for we remain ever mindful of our own far greater forgiven debt.

When we withhold forgiveness, we remain tethered to

past injuries, allowing them to shape our present and future. We inadvertently grant continuing power to those who have wounded us, permitting them to exert influence long after the initial offense. Paradoxically, the act of forgiveness liberates not primarily the forgiven but the forgiver.

Eternal debtors who have internalized their identity possess a remarkable psychological resilience. Affronts and injuries, rather than triggering indignation, evoke remembrance of their own forgiven state. This perspective transforms potential conflicts into opportunities to participate in the divine pattern of mercy.

CONTEMPORARY APPLICATION

This biblical principle maintains its relevance in modern contexts. We frequently encounter situations where:

- We receive divine forgiveness for significant transgressions against God's perfect standard.

- We face opportunities to forgive others for relatively minor offenses compared to our own spiritual debts.

- We must choose between strict justice and merciful forgiveness.

Even when circumstances appear to justify withholding forgiveness—whether due to financial hardship, extended periods of injury, or legitimate grievances—the divine mandate remains unchanged. The obligation to forgive transcends human justification for withholding it.

Our identity as eternal debtors provides the necessary framework for navigating these complex situations. When tempted to withhold forgiveness due to the severity of an offense, we recall the incomparably greater debt from which we have been released. When our hearts resist extending mercy, we remember our fundamental position as recipients of mercy.

Consider the example of one who has suffered profound betrayal by a spouse, business partner, or close friend. Human wisdom might counsel caution, self-protection, or even righteous indignation. Divine wisdom, however, calls us to a higher standard—not because the offense was insignificant, but precisely because our own need for forgiveness is so immense.

THE ECONOMICS OF HEAVENLY FORGIVENESS

The concept of eternal indebtedness reveals a divine economy operating on principles radically different from earthly economics. In human financial systems, debts must be repaid for the system to function; in the heavenly economy, debts are forgiven as the normal course of operation.

This inverted economic model challenges our innate sense of transactional justice. We instinctively believe that debts should be collected, not forgiven; that accounts should balance through equivalent exchange, not unilateral clemency. The parable of the unmerciful servant confronts these assumptions directly, proposing an alternative economic paradigm where forgiveness— not repayment—becomes the primary currency.

In this divine economy, we discover several counterintuitive principles:

1. **Wealth Through Release:** We become spiritually wealthy not by collecting what others owe us, but by releasing them from their obligations.

2. **Abundance Through Giving:** Our supply of forgiveness increases rather than diminishes through its liberal distribution.

3. **Security Through Surrender:** We establish our place in this economy not by demanding our rights, but by relinquishing them.

These principles, while seemingly impractical in worldly terms, form the operational basis of the Kingdom of God. When Jesus taught His disciples to pray, "Forgive us our debts, as we forgive our debtors" (Matthew 6:12), He was not merely offering a spiritual platitude but articulating the fundamental economic principle of His kingdom.

FORGIVENESS AND JUSTICE

A common misconception equates forgiveness with the abandonment of justice. This overlooks the complex relationship between mercy and accountability. Forgiveness does not necessarily negate consequences; rather, it releases the forgiver from the burden of administering those consequences personally.

For the eternal debtor, this distinction proves crucial. We can forgive genuinely while still acknowledging the objective reality of wrongdoing. We can release offenders from our personal judgment while still recognizing the legitimate authority of established justice systems. We can surrender our right to vengeance while still participating in processes of accountability and restoration.

When we forgive, we essentially transfer the case from our limited jurisdiction to God's perfect court. As Paul writes in Romans 12:19: "Beloved, never avenge yourselves, but leave room for the wrath of God; for it is written, 'Vengeance is mine, I will repay, says the Lord.'"

This perspective allows us to pursue both forgiveness and appropriate boundaries. We can release offenders from our personal judgment while still implementing necessary protections and systemic reforms. Forgiveness operates on the spiritual and emotional plane, while accountability functions in the practical and relational dimensions.

THE PRACTICE OF FORGIVENESS FOR ETERNAL DEBTORS

The practice of forgiveness represents more than a moral imperative; it constitutes a fundamental condition for receiving divine mercy. As beneficiaries of God's boundless forgiveness, we bear the responsibility to extend similar grace to others. This principle encourages tempering justice with mercy, following the example set by the King of Kings in His dealings with humanity.

When confronted with opportunities to exact retribution or teach harsh lessons, we must remember our position as recipients of divine mercy. Our response should reflect the same generous spirit of forgiveness that we have received.

For the eternal debtor, forgiveness becomes not an occasional act but a perpetual posture—a constant readiness to extend to others what we ourselves continually require. This posture manifests in several practical ways:

1. **Preemptive Forgiveness**: Developing a disposition to forgive even before offense occurs.

2. **Prompt Forgiveness**: Addressing injuries quickly before resentment can take root.

3. **Persistent Forgiveness**: Continuing to forgive when memories of past wounds resurface.

4. **Progressive Forgiveness**: Recognizing forgiveness as an ongoing process rather than a single event.

Practically speaking, forgiveness often unfolds as a process rather than a single event. For profound injuries, we may need to forgive repeatedly, each time surrendering our right to resentment anew. This ongoing surrender gradually transforms our hearts until forgiveness becomes less an arduous duty and more a reflexive expression of our redeemed nature.

THE TRANSFORMATIVE POWER OF EMBRACING ETERNAL INDEBTEDNESS

Perhaps counterintuitively, embracing our identity as eternal debtors produces not shame but liberation. When we acknowledge the magnitude of our forgiven debt, several transformative shifts occur:

1. **From Entitlement to Gratitude**: We move from demanding what we deserve to marveling at what we've received despite our unworthiness.

2. **From Judgment to Compassion**: We view others not through the lens of their failures but through awareness of our own forgiven faults.

3. **From Scarcity to Abundance**: We operate not from fear of insufficient grace but from confidence in its inexhaustible supply.

4. **From Performance to Reception**: We cease striving to earn what can only be received as gift.

This transformed perspective alters not only how we forgive but how we live entirely. The eternal debtor paradoxically experiences profound freedom—released from the exhausting pretense of moral self-sufficiency and the crushing burden of maintaining spiritual ledgers.

CONCLUSION

In the final analysis, our willingness to forgive reveals whether we have truly grasped the magnitude of our own forgiveness. It demonstrates whether the economy of grace has merely informed our theology or fundamentally transformed our hearts.

The concept of eternal indebtedness, far from diminishing human dignity, actually establishes our true worth in divine terms. Our value derives not from what we can repay but from what God was willing to forgive—not from our assets but from the price paid to clear our liabilities. This inverted value system forms the foundation of Christian identity and the wellspring of Christian forgiveness.

As eternal debtors in the economy of divine grace, we discover a profound truth: in the Kingdom of God, acknowledged bankruptcy becomes the prerequisite for immeasurable wealth. When we embrace our identity as those forgiven much, we gain both the capacity and the motivation to love much extending to others the same mercy that continually sustains us.

"Therefore, I tell you, her many sins have been forgiven—as her great love has shown. But whoever has been forgiven little loves little." (Luke 7:47)

Chapter 13

REVENGE

One of the dangers of offense is seeking an opportunity to get even. We can be overwhelmed with pain to an immeasurable degree, to the point where revenge seems like a good outlet to vent our frustrations and pain. However, seeking to do wrong, inflict pain, or wish evil on someone so that your feelings are justified is not our place as Christians. Here are some reasons why God does not want us to seek revenge:

- When we seek revenge, we pass judgment. God is the only righteous judge, so we must leave judgment to Him.

- Revenge is the fruit of anger, and James 1:20 tells us, "The anger of man does not produce the righteousness of God."

- Revenge leads to sin.

- Revenge is seeking to destroy. It does not aim to build, correct, or win back.

- Anyone who seeks revenge has been overcome with evil.

"Beloved, never avenge yourselves, but leave it to the wrath of God; for it is written, 'Vengeance is mine, I will repay,' says the Lord." — Romans 12:19

"Do not be overcome by evil but overcome evil with good." — Romans 12:21

No matter how bad things are or how tough you may think you are, trust me when I say this: God can avenge you far better than you could ever avenge yourself. He can fight for you more effectively than you could fight for yourself.

Can you imagine having God as an enemy? I don't know about you, but I don't want anything to do with that possibility. Do you even understand what it means when the Bible says, "Avenge not yourselves; I will repay"?

We often interpret this scripture to mean that God punishes the offender, which is true—He does that in some cases. But don't forget that God is also a mediator.

So, God not only punishes the offender, but He also corrects the offender. By this scripture, He essentially says:

"I apologize for My son or daughter who wronged you. Leave them to Me; I'll take care of them." Then, He compensates you for the wrong you suffered at the hands of the offender. Walking with God for a few years now has taught me that He corrects and convicts far more often than He punishes. It is our earnest desire that God punishes people severely so they will learn a lesson, but I have learned another important lesson about God: some convictions are more painful than punishment.

There is an adage in my local language that says, "If you know how to talk, God will not talk for you, and if you know how to fight, God will not fight your battles for you." So leave everything to God. Don't seek revenge. It is vain and weak because it accomplishes nothing but destruction. It gives the devil a foothold in your life, and the devil uses that to manipulate you. Revenge consumes you with anger and overwhelms you with pain. In those moments, retaliation seems like the best answer. Don't give in to it. You will feel condemned and guilty immediately after you have exacted revenge.

THE PRICE OF REVENGE

Consider the story of Absalom in the Bible. I encourage you to read the story in 2 Samuel 13-18. This story serves as a powerful cautionary tale about how revenge, even when motivated by a legitimate grievance (like Tamar's assault), can set in motion events that spiral far beyond the original intention, ultimately consuming the person seeking vengeance. In Absalom's case, what began as a brother defending his sister's honor ended with his death, a devastated father, and a divided kingdom.

The narrative raises profound questions about justice versus vengeance and how seeking personal revenge, rather than trusting divine or legal justice, can lead to tragic outcomes that far outweigh the initial offense. It's particularly poignant that David's grief over Absalom's death suggests that even after everything that happened, reconciliation might have been possible had revenge not driven them so far apart.

A retrospective study of Absalom's life indicates that his demise can be attributed to one trait: revenge. A prospective study tells us that there is a direct correlation between revenge and destruction. Revenge, even when justified, can be destructive. It is only a matter of time before you spiral out of control. Revenge makes you feel justified, but vengeance leads to more violence.

"Then Jesus said to him, 'Put your sword back into its place; for all who take the sword will perish by the sword.'" — Matthew 26:52

This statement to Peter tells us that even "justified" revenge can lead to destructive outcomes. There is a scripture that always blows my mind when I think of it. God does not want you to take matters into your own hands. When God sees you rejoicing over someone He is punishing, He may stop punishing the person because of your attitude.

"Rejoice not when thine enemy falleth and let not thine heart be glad when he stumbleth: lest the Lord see it, and it displease Him, and He turn away His wrath from him." — Proverbs 24:17-18, KJV

THE ATTITUDE TOWARD ENEMIES

This scripture offers an important lesson on humility, mercy, and the attitude believers should have toward those who oppose them. It highlights several key principles:

1. **Avoid vindictiveness:** This verse instructs us not to take pleasure in the misfortune or downfall of our enemies. While it is natural to feel some satisfaction when those who oppose us face difficulties, this passage cautions against rejoicing in their suffering.

Instead, it encourages us to rise above personal grievances and show compassion, even toward those who have wronged us.

2. **God's perspective:** The passage makes it clear that when we delight in the downfall of others, it displeases God. It suggests that God sees our hearts and the attitudes we harbor. Such feelings are not in alignment with His will and could even lead to God redirecting His judgment away from the enemy—an ironic reversal of what we may have hoped for.

3. **Mercy and grace:** This passage aligns with the broader biblical themes of mercy and forgiveness. Just as God shows mercy to us, we are encouraged to extend mercy to others, even to those who consider us enemies, aligning ourselves with God's heart and demonstrating a Christ-like attitude of grace.

4. **Trust in God's justice:** Proverbs 24:17-18 reminds us that justice belongs to God, not to us. Rather than finding pleasure in the punishment of others, we are called to trust in God's perfect judgment and timing. He is sovereign and will address wrongs in His way and at the right time. It is not our place to usurp His authority by delighting in the misfortunes of others.

These verses encourage believers to adopt a posture of humility, mercy, and trust in God's justice, avoiding vengeful or spiteful attitudes. They challenge us to rise above personal grievances and reflect God's heart of forgiveness and mercy in all our interactions with others.

If you want your enemies to experience the full wrath of God, don't gloat over their downfall. Act as though you don't even know God is punishing them. In this way, God can do what He does best. I just gave you a mean but godly piece of advice—they will experience the full weight and wrath of God.

DON'T LET REVENGE BLOCK POSSIBLE PATHS OF RECONCILIATION

Absalom killed Amnon for raping Tamar, setting off a cascade of devastating consequences. While his desire for justice for his sister was understandable, his choice to take matters into his own hands through murder initiated a tragic chain of events. Revenge forced Absalom into exile, strained his relationship with his father, fractured his family, led to rebellion—seeking his father's throne, and ultimately resulted in his death.

HEAVEN'S LEGAL SYSTEM

"For the Lord is our judge, the Lord is our lawgiver, the Lord is our king; he will save us." — Isaiah 33:22

This verse from Isaiah 33:22 presents an interesting parallel to the concept of separated governmental powers. Let me explore each aspect:

- **The Lord as Judge (Judiciary):** This portrays God as the ultimate arbiter of justice, determining right from wrong and rendering decisions with perfect wisdom and fairness. Like a judicial branch, this role involves interpreting and applying the law to specific cases, but with divine perfect knowledge and complete impartiality.

- **The Lord as Lawgiver (Legislature):** This depicts God as the source of moral and spiritual law, establishing the standards and principles by which people should live. Like legislature, this role involves creating and establishing laws. However, in this case, they are divine commandments rather than human statutes. The Ten Commandments would be a prime example of this legislative function.

- **The Lord as King (Executive):** This presents God as the sovereign ruler who implements and enforces the laws. Like an executive branch, this role involves leadership and governance, ensuring the laws are carried out and protected. However, unlike earthly executives, God's authority is absolute and eternal.

It's fascinating how this ancient text presents a unified but multi-faceted view of divine authority that parallels what would later become known as the separation of powers in modern governance. However, while human governments separate these powers to prevent abuse and provide checks and balances, in this religious context, they are perfectly united in one divine being who is considered incapable of error or corruption.

The final phrase, "he will save us," adds another dimension beyond governmental structure, suggesting that these roles serve not just for governance but also for redemption and protection of the governed. Trust this infallible legal system to avenge you.

THE LAW OF RETALIATION

A law can be defined as the system of rules that a particular country or community recognizes as regulating the actions of its members and which it may enforce by imposing penalties. These laws are often established and enforced by local or international institutions and governing bodies. In some instances, life was sought for life, but the true essence of having laws is to prevent individuals from taking matters into their own hands. Laws are also meant to set boundaries and ensure that punishment is fair and not arbitrary.

The principle of "an eye for an eye, a tooth for a tooth, a life for a life" is a foundational concept in ancient legal systems that sought to establish equitable justice through proportional punishment. Originating in the Code of

Hammurabi from Mesopotamia, this principle emerged as a sophisticated approach to resolving conflicts and maintaining social order.

Fundamentally, the concept aimed to limit retributive violence by prescribing punishments that directly corresponded to the harm committed. This legal framework represented a significant advancement from earlier systems of blood feuds and unlimited vengeance, introducing a structured method of achieving justice.

In its biblical context, found in the Book of Exodus, the principle was paradoxically designed to restrict excessive punishment rather than encourage brutal retaliation. It provided a legal ceiling for consequences, preventing escalating cycles of violence between individuals and communities.

Modern legal and philosophical thought has largely moved beyond literal interpretation. Influential thinkers like Mahatma Gandhi critiqued the concept, arguing that true justice requires compassion, rehabilitation, and the breaking of cycles of violence rather than perpetuating them through mechanical retribution.

Contemporary justice systems reflect this evolved understanding, emphasizing proportionality, rehabilitation, and social restoration over pure punitive measures. The ancient principle remains a critical historical milestone in humanity's ongoing journey to create fair and humane systems of legal accountability.

The core intent was to create a systematic approach to justice that prevented endless cycles of escalating violence by establishing clear, predictable consequences for criminal actions.

An eye for an eye is descriptive of the extent to which punishment is to be measured out to people found liable for an offense, but Proverbs 25:21 gives us a prescriptive law of retaliation: "If thine enemy be hungry, give him bread to eat; and if he be thirsty, give him water to drink: For thou shalt heap coals of fire upon his head, and the Lord shall reward thee."

This passage from Proverbs 25:21-22 presents a profound ethical teaching about responding to an enemy's suffering with compassion. The instruction to feed and give drink to one's hungry and thirsty enemy challenges natural human instincts of retaliation.

The metaphorical "heap coals of fire upon his head" is not about literal punishment but a symbolic representation of transformative kindness. This phrase is likely meant to invoke shame or conscience in the enemy through unexpected mercy. By responding to hostility with generosity, one might provoke profound moral reflection and potential reconciliation.

The text suggests that divine reward comes not through vengeance but through radical acts of compassion. It advocates for breaking cycles of hatred by responding to animosity with unexpected kindness, potentially converting an enemy through grace rather than retribution.

This teaching aligns with broader biblical principles of loving one's enemies and overcoming evil with good, presenting a counterintuitive approach to conflict that prioritizes human dignity and potential transformation over immediate satisfaction or revenge.

Chapter 14

INTERNALIZING VS. VOCALIZING

When asked, "How are you doing?" we often default to the answer, "I am fine," even when we are not. We try to contain everything and suppress many of our emotions, often to keep appearances. However, when you're not feeling well, it is important to seek counsel. If you need someone to talk to, find a person who offers godly counsel and someone you can trust.

While it's wise to keep certain things private—you don't want to reveal too much of your personal life to outsiders, nor do you want everyone to know what's going on in your world—there's a limit to how much we can internalize. People, I find, are like rubber bands. We have our elasticity limits, and when stretched past those limits, we sometimes snap. That's because there is only so much, we can take as individuals. Internalizing too much can become detrimental to our sanity, spirituality, and even our health.

We want to keep a tight lid on everything, and sometimes that's good, but other times, it's not. Consider what happens when you shake a carbonated drink like Coca-Cola or Pepsi; pressure builds inside until it either bursts open the bottle or gushes out forcefully when the lid is opened. Similarly, a glass bottle left in the freezer can burst because the molecules expand. That's what happens to us when we internalize more than we can handle.

If you need to talk, find someone you can:

- Trust – You need someone who will tell you the truth, not just what you want to hear, and someone who genuinely cares for you.

- Confide in – Avoid people who have loose tongues or gossip about others.

There are people you love and trust, but not all of them are people you can confide in. I pray for discernment in this matter.

Be vocal but avoid talking to miserable people. As the saying goes, misery loves company. Some people may be dealing with bad experiences or rough seasons in life, and when you open up to them, they may project their problems onto you, making you feel as though you have the same problem they do. Be careful not to let others' problems create problems you don't have.

You don't need a pity party to validate your feelings or issues. Instead, seek good counsel, positive influences, and positive vibes—as they say. Spending time with offended people can make you like them. If you surround yourself with complainers, you'll start complaining, too. For instance, friends who constantly criticize their spouses may influence you to complain about yours. Avoid offended people.

Don't internalize your issues; vocalize them. Make sure your concerns are heard so that, if correction is needed, it can be offered. Vocalizing helps ensure that misunderstandings are addressed, perceptions are corrected, and offenders are made aware that their words or actions were noted and not appreciated.

AT HOME WITH MARY AND MARTHA

"Now as they went on their way, he entered a village; and a woman named Martha received him into her house. And she had a sister called Mary, who sat at the Lord's feet and listened to His teaching. But Martha was distracted with much serving; and she went to Him and said, 'Lord, do you not care that my

sister has left me to serve alone? Tell her then to help me.' But the Lord answered her, 'Martha, Martha, you are anxious and troubled about many things; one thing is needful. Mary has chosen the good portion, which shall not be taken away from her.'"
— Luke 10:38–42

In this scripture, Jesus visits the home of two sisters, Mary and Martha. Martha, focused on service and hospitality, was ensuring everything was in place—food, water, and everything else that the visitors would need. Meanwhile, her sister Mary sat at Jesus' feet, listening to His teaching.

Overwhelmed by her responsibilities and the lack of assistance from Mary, Martha admonished Jesus, asking Him to tell Mary to help. Jesus, however, responded by acknowledging Martha's anxiety without downplaying the relevance of hospitality or service. He pointed out that Mary had chosen the most important priority: building a relationship with Him and learning from Him.

Had Martha internalized her frustration at Mary; those feelings of offense could have consumed her. By vocalizing her concerns, Martha opened the door for Jesus to guide her, correct her perceptions, and alleviate her anxiety.

Whenever you're feeling something or thinking a particular thought about someone, it's important to express it. Open communication allows for clarification and prevents misunderstandings, after all, nobody is a mind reader. If there were ever a job called "mind reader," it would undoubtedly be the highest-paying role in the world, given how tough it would be. Imagine driving on a highway where cars lack turn signals—we wouldn't know who intends to turn left or right. In the same way, people cannot discern your thoughts or emotions unless you share them.

By vocalizing her feelings, Martha created an opportunity for correction, guidance, and realignment of her priorities. It became a teaching moment that has benefited believers for generations. More importantly, she achieved emotional resolution rather than allowing resentment to fester.

Jesus acknowledged her feelings but did not validate them.

This is a critical lesson for our generation: we must be careful about how we validate feelings. While feelings are subjective and personal making, it's essential to recognize that they can also be deceptive, manipulative, blinding, and capable of leading us astray.

Because we cannot expect others to read our minds, clear communication is vital to prevent misunderstandings. Suppressing your emotions are unhealthy for any relationship. On the other hand, expressing emotions in a healthy way builds better and stronger relationships. Even seemingly negative experiences and emotions provide learning opportunities that make for growth and maturity.

Chapter 15

LOVE

"You have heard that it has been said, 'You shall love your neighbor and hate your enemy.' But I say unto you, love your enemies, bless them that curse you, do good to them that hate you, and pray for them which despitefully use you and persecute you."

These words of Jesus, immortalized in Matthew 5:43-44, present a challenge that transcends the boundaries of human nature. This command doesn't merely ask us to love those who are easy to love—our family, friends, and allies—but extends to those we might consider enemies: those who hurt us, curse us, and persecute us. At first glance, such a command seems not just difficult but impossible. Human nature rebels against showing kindness to those who have wronged us. Yet, the gospel reveals that through the transformative power of the Holy Spirit, this kind of love is not only possible—it becomes our new reality.

Loving our enemies isn't about manufacturing feelings of affection or goodwill toward those who oppose us. It's about choosing a response that honors God, regardless of our feelings. The call to love challenges our natural inclinations and invites us to love with the same depth and constancy that Jesus exhibited. When we reflect on how challenging it can be to love even those closest to us, how often we fail those dearests to our hearts—the task of loving our enemies appears even more daunting. But it's precisely this challenge that illuminates our desperate need for divine intervention in our hearts.

Through the Holy Spirit's power, we become equipped to love beyond human limitations. Paul affirms this truth in Romans 5:5: "And hope does not put us to shame, because the love of God has been poured out into our hearts through the Holy Spirit, who has been given to us." This supernatural love enables us to extend grace even when it seems undeserved, to bless those who curse us, and to pray sincerely for those who mistreat and persecute us.

The love Jesus presents isn't conditional. It doesn't depend on the recipient's actions or behavior but flows freely, mirroring God's love for us. As 2 Peter 1:2-4 reminds us: "Grace and peace be multiplied unto you through the knowledge of God and of Jesus our Lord." Our capacity to love as Christ loved expands as we deepen our knowledge of Him. The more profoundly we understand the magnitude of His love for us—despite our flaws, sins, and failures, the more compelled we feel to extend that same love to others, including those who have wounded us. Grace and peace multiply within us as our relationship with Christ deepens, allowing His transformative love to remake our hearts and empower us to love as He does.

In John 13:34-35, Jesus provides another profound directive: "A new commandment I give to you, that you love one another: just as I have loved you, you also are to love one another. By this all people will know that you are my disciples, if you have love for one another." Jesus' love wasn't constrained by others' behavior. He loved even those who betrayed, denied, and abandoned Him. His love remained unconditional, sacrificial, and enduring. The command to love others "as I have loved you" establishes a profound standard. It requires not just a willingness to forgive but a deep, abiding commitment to care for others, even when doing so proves costly or difficult. The qualification "as I have loved you" calls us beyond surface-level affection to embody the sacrificial love that Jesus demonstrated.

Living out this command can be challenging, especially in difficult relationships or circumstances. The journey toward loving like Jesus doesn't happen overnight. It requires persistent effort, daily prayer, and a commitment to meditation on God's Word. As we seek to love like Jesus, we must remember that this love isn't rooted in fleeting emotions but in obedience to God's command. It doesn't ignore sin but seeks to cover it with grace, as 1 Peter 4:8 reminds us: "Above all, keep loving one another earnestly, since love covers a multitude of sins." While this kind of love may not prevent sin, it possesses the power to heal relationships, bring reconciliation, and break cycles of bitterness that perpetuate harm.

In practical terms, Jesus' teaching calls us to transform our responses to people and situations that test us most severely. Consider a colleague who consistently undermines your efforts or a family member who has inflicted deep wounds. Our instinct might be to harbor resentment or seek revenge. Yet Christ commands us to walk a different path.

First, we can begin by praying for their well-being and asking God to bless them, even when doing so feels impossible. This act of prayer shifts our focus from our hurt to their needs, aligning our hearts with God's desire for reconciliation and peace.

Second, we are called to practice speaking grace when discussing them with others. Instead of gossiping or venting bitterness, we can choose words that reflect Christ's kindness. We can highlight their positive qualities and refrain from amplifying their flaws.

Lastly, we can seek practical ways to demonstrate kindness. If a colleague struggles with a project, we can help. If someone spreads gossip about us, we can respond by emphasizing their strengths in conversations with others. These actions, though initially difficult, can gradually soften our hearts and reflect love's transformative power.

The journey toward loving like Jesus requires persistence and willingness to allow the Holy Spirit to reshape our hearts. Loving those who hurt us rarely comes easily, but through consistent practice, prayer, and obedience, we draw closer to embodying Christ's love. This journey, though challenging, begins with small steps—heartfelt prayers, kind words, and acts of grace. Over time, these seemingly insignificant actions reshape our hearts, helping us become more like the One who loved us first, even while we were still His enemies.

In a world fragmented by division and hostility, this radical love stands as a testament to the gospel's transformative power. When we love our enemies, we don't merely obey a command—we participate in God's redemptive work, offering glimpses of His kingdom breaking into our broken world. And perhaps most remarkably, as we extend this supernatural love to others, we ourselves are transformed, discovering freedom from bitterness and experiencing the profound joy that comes from walking in obedience to our Savior's call.

Chapter 16

BRIDLE THE CULPRIT

Imagine a body without a tongue. Without this vital organ, verbal communication would be impossible— we would be forced to write everything down, forever missing the sweet cadence of each other's voices. Joyful celebrations would lack the sounds of laughter and cheers. We would be deprived of the melodious songs, orchestral symphonies, and world-renowned classics that breathe life into our most precious moments. Without our tongues, our taste buds would never experience the symphony of flavors that set our mouths ablaze during meals shared with beloved friends and family.

Yet coupled with these magnificent benefits comes an awesome responsibility—the ability to utter words that carry immense power:

- Blessings and curses

- Kindness and offense

- Joy and sorrow

- Building and breaking

The tongue stands as one of the most influential members of the human body. It possesses the power to elevate or destroy, to create harmony or sow discord. James 1:26 reminds us: "If you claim to be religious but don't control your tongue, you are fooling yourself, and your religion is worthless."

This represents an area where all of us can improve. Many have experienced the sting of saying the wrong thing: words that slipped out unintentionally or were misinterpreted. Even statements offered with the best intentions can be communicated poorly or received incorrectly, causing unintended harm. We must exercise vigilant caution in our speech and remember that, like spilled water, once words flow forth, they cannot be gathered back.

We can apologize for what we say, but sometimes the damage or hurt caused by our statements extends beyond repair. Restraint in speech is essential. Too often in our daily lives and relationships with family and friends, we encounter those who defend their harsh words with phrases like, "That's just who I am," or "I need to get this off my chest so I can feel better," or the ever popular, "I have to be real with you." While honesty certainly has its place, we should never become known as brash or loose talkers.

You may struggle valiantly to refute an impression created by your careless words, but it may be too late. While some damage can be managed or controlled, once spoken, words leave an indelible impact. Even after a sincere apology, complete acceptance of responsibility, and full recantation, the memory of those words remains. The ability to withhold impulsive speech—to resist the urge to blurt out every passing thought—represents a hallmark of maturity and self-control. This isn't about pretending or being disingenuous; rather, it's about exercising wisdom, maturity, self-discipline, and grace in our communication.

Those who speak excessively or lack discretion inevitably fall into sin or cause offense. Proverbs 10:19 articulates this truth with elegant precision:

"In the multitude of words, sin is not lacking, but the person who restrains his lips is wise."

This verse reveals a profound truth about the relationship between excessive speech and wisdom. A

161

multitude of words increases the likelihood of sin—whether through gossip, exaggeration, boasting, or speaking without proper reflection. The more we talk, the greater the possibility that we'll say something harmful or offensive. However, Scripture makes it clear that exercising restraint in speech is a mark of wisdom.

This verse does not advocate monastic silence but rather encourages thoughtful communication. The wise person understands that every word carries weight and potential consequences, so they choose to speak with purpose and discretion rather than allowing words to flow unchecked.

This principle extends far beyond spoken words to encompass what we type in text messages, messaging apps, and social media. Careless or offensive digital communication can inflict as much harm as spoken words. Just as we must be cautious with our speech, we must exercise equal restraint and intentionality in our digital interactions.

WHAT I SAID VERSUS WHAT YOU HEARD

These concepts reveal greater complexity than their surface appearance suggests. Countless instances arise when meaning gets lost in translation, and we misinterpret the words or intentions of others.

Misinterpretations in communication stem from various factors, including ambiguity in language, tone of voice, cultural differences, emotional states, lack of active listening, misreading of nonverbal cues, and lack of clarity or precision. By understanding these causes and striving to communicate more clearly and thoughtfully, we can reduce misunderstandings and enhance the effectiveness of our communication.

AMBIGUITY IN LANGUAGE

Ambiguity in language stands as a primary cause of misinterpretation. Words and phrases often carry multiple meanings depending on context, leading to confusion. For instance, the word "bank" might refer to a financial institution or the side of a river. Similarly, vague or generalized statements leave room for varying interpretations. A comment like "We should work on this soon" might be understood as "later today," "this week," or even "whenever we get to it," depending on the listener's perception. Such ambiguity results in mismatched expectations and actions.

TONE OF VOICE

The tone of voice plays a crucial role in how messages are received. The emotional tenor in which something is expressed can dramatically alter its meaning. For example, "Oh, great!" spoken with enthusiasm conveys excitement, while the same phrase delivered with sarcasm communicates frustration. Misunderstanding the speaker's tone can lead to misinterpretation of their intentions or feelings.

CULTURAL DIFFERENCES

Cultural differences represent another common source of misinterpretation. People from different cultural backgrounds often interpret words, actions, and non-verbal cues through distinct lenses. For instance, maintaining eye contact is considered a sign of confidence and respect in some cultures, while in others, it may be perceived as rude or confrontational. Failing to recognize these differences can lead to misunderstandings, as what one culture considers respectful might be received negatively in another.

EMOTIONAL STATES

Emotional states can profoundly distort both the delivery and interpretation of messages. When experiencing strong emotions, whether anger, frustration, or excitement, our ability to convey or interpret information becomes impaired. Strong emotions can exaggerate the perceived meaning of a message or cause us to misinterpret neutral statements. An angry person might perceive a simple suggestion as harsh criticism, while an excited individual might interpret a neutral comment as enthusiastic support.

LACK OF ACTIVE LISTENING

Miscommunication frequently occurs when people fail to engage in active listening. Often, we find ourselves distracted or only partially engaged in conversation, missing critical details. When not actively listening, we tend to fill in gaps with our assumptions, which may not align with the speaker's intended message. This happens when, for example, someone is mentally elsewhere while their colleague explains a problem, resulting in advice that doesn't address the actual issue because key details weren't absorbed.

NONVERBAL CUES

Nonverbal cues—body language, facial expressions, and gestures—add vital context to verbal communication. However, misreading these cues leads to misunderstanding. For instance, folded arms might appear defensive or disinterested, even if the person is simply cold or tired. Misinterpreting these nonverbal signals can create a false perception that the speaker is insincere or hostile when that is not the case.

LACK OF CLARITY OR PRECISION

A lack of clarity or precision in communication inevitably creates confusion. When thoughts aren't articulated clearly, either due to poor preparation or an assumption that others will understand, misinterpretations become likely. For example, saying "I'm not sure" could be taken as uncertainty about facts, whereas "I don't have enough information to make a decision yet" provides a clearer picture of the speaker's position.

Clear and intentional communication forms the foundation of healthy relationships. Suppressed emotions and careless words damage trust and create barriers between people. Whether spoken aloud or written down, our words should reflect wisdom, self-control, and grace. While misunderstandings are inevitable in human interaction, by striving for clarity and thoughtful communication, we can minimize their occurrence and strengthen our connections with others.

Let our communication reflect the love, maturity, and discernment that transcends ordinary conversation—elevating our interactions to something that builds up rather than tears down, that unites rather than divides, that heals rather than wounds.

Chapter 17

PRIDE

The ancient Greeks had a word for it: *hubris*. That dangerous elevation of self that preceded the fall of heroes and kings alike. We moderns call it pride—a word that shimmers with contradiction, capable of both elevating our humanity and destroying it entirely.

THE DUAL NATURE OF PRIDE

Pride stands at the crossroads of virtue and vice, wearing two faces that look nothing alike.

In its nobler form, pride manifests as self-respect, that quiet dignity that allows us to stand tall in a world that would often prefer we kneel. It's the warm glow of satisfaction when we overcome, achieve, and grow beyond our former limitations. This healthy pride is the soil from which self-worth blooms, setting necessary boundaries and establishing our place in the constellation of human relationships.

Consider the graduate who walks across the stage after years of predawn study sessions and midnight oil burned. The single mother who, against all odds, builds a life of stability for her children. The artist who finally captures on canvas what has lived only in imagination. Their pride is not a sin but a testament—a recognition that something worthy has been accomplished through perseverance and courage.

This kind of pride:

- Extends its hand to lift others, finding joy in contribution rather than competition

- Stands secure enough in its own accomplishments to celebrate the triumphs of others

- Acknowledges every helping hand that made success possible

- Walks hand-in-hand with humility, knowing how easily it all could have gone another way

THE SHADOW SIDE

But pride has a darker twin—what the ancients called self-conceit. This is pride corrupted, twisted into something unrecognizable from its healthier counterpart.

In the quiet chambers of psychology, self-conceit is understood as a fundamental misapprehension—the belief that one exists at the center of the universe, uniquely valuable beyond all others. It manifests as that unmistakable air of superiority that enters a room before the person does. The patronizing tone that makes a simple conversation feel like an audience granted. The dismissive glance that renders others invisible.

Here lies pride's most insidious danger: its remarkable ability to camouflage itself within our psyche. How easily we spot it in others—the arrogant boss, the condescending friend, the self-important stranger—while remaining blind to its presence in ourselves. Like a virus that disables the body's warning systems, pride convinces us we are immune to its influence even as it reshapes our character.

THE FIVE "I WILLS"

Ancient wisdom records the first fall from grace with devastating simplicity. Before Lucifer became Satan, before paradise was lost, there was a sequence of fatal declarations—five statements that transformed the light-bearer into darkness incarnate:

"I will ascend into heaven." "I will exalt my throne above the stars of God." "I will also sit on the mount of the congregation." "I will ascend above the heights of the clouds." "I will be like the Most High."

Notice the pattern—the relentless "I" that bends reality around itself like a black hole, drawing all things into its gravity. What began as beauty ended in destruction, all because of five whispered assertions of self-importance.

Before dismissing this as mere mythology, consider how these five "I Wills" echo in the chambers of your own heart. Ask yourself:

Do you quietly believe your judgment is superior to all others? Must you have the final word in every significant discussion? Would you sacrifice relationship on the altar of being right? Do your needs and desires consistently take precedence over others'? Do warnings and counsel bounce off your certainty like rain off stone? Does surrender of control feel like surrender of self? Have you surrounded yourself only with those who pose no threat to your sense of superiority?

If you answered "no" to all of these, congratulations—you may be the proudest person reading these words. The truly proud never recognize their condition.

ATTRIBUTES OF SINFUL PRIDE

This corrupted pride leaves distinctive fingerprints wherever it touches:

It requires an inflated self-image, maintained through careful curation and selective attention. It creates a zero-sum game where another's success feels like personal failure. It develops selective blindness to the strengths and contributions of others. It possesses microscopic vision for flaws in others, telescopic vision for their own virtues. It transforms life into an endless competition where second place equals last. It cultivates an inflated and fragile ego.

THE PRIDE OF LIFE

"For all that is in the world—the lust of the flesh, the lust of the eyes, and the pride of life—is not of the Father but is of the world." These ancient words from 1 John 2:16 identified three perennial temptations, with pride taking its place as perhaps the most subtle and dangerous.

The original Greek term, *alazoneia tou biou*, carries the weight of pretentiousness—a boastful trumpeting of one's importance and accomplishments. It describes the misplaced confidence in things that are passing away: status that will fade, achievements that will be forgotten, possessions that will eventually belong to others.

This "pride of life" manifests when we derive our sense of worth from temporal markers:

- The prestigious title on your business card

- The exclusive address on your mail

- The designer label hidden inside your collar

- The connections you casually mention in conversation

- The reservation at the restaurant where tables are scarce

None inherently evil, all potentially deadly—not because of what they are, but because of what they become when they form the foundation of our identity and worth.

What if we redirected that instinct to boast toward something more substantial? What if your pride came not from what you possess but from what you give. Not from your accumulation but your contribution.

Not from the titles you've earned but the lives you've touched. This represents a profound reorientation of the human spirit—from the temporary toward the eternal.

THE END OF PRIDE

"Pride goes before destruction, and a haughty spirit before fall." These words from Proverbs 16:18 have echoed through centuries, not because they represent wishful moralism, but because they describe an observable pattern woven into the fabric of human experience.

The Hebrew poet uses parallel terms—*ga'own* (pride) and *gobah ruach* (haughty spirit)—to emphasize the inevitability of pride's consequences. This isn't punishment so much as natural law. Pride creates the conditions for its own downfall by distorting our perception: minimizing risks, overestimating abilities, dismissing wisdom, and alienating allies.

This ancient wisdom resonates across diverse traditions: "God opposes the proud but gives grace to the humble." (James 4:6) "When pride comes, then comes disgrace." (Proverbs 11:2) "Whoever exalts himself will be humbled." (Matthew 23:12)

History serves as pride's ledger, recording its devastating

consequences in the rise and fall of empires, the tragic arcs of leaders, and the wreckage of countless personal relationships. From Ozymandias to Napoleon, from Enron to Theranos, pride leaves the same signature on its victims—a blindness that precedes the fall.

PRIDE IS EASILY OFFENDED

Among pride's most reliable symptoms is hypersensitivity—a hair-trigger response to perceived slights and challenges. For the proud person, minor criticisms feel like major assaults. Gentle suggestions become intolerable insults. Innocent oversights transform into deliberate disrespect.

This quickness to take offense reveals pride's fundamental insecurity. Despite its posture of strength, it remains perpetually defensive, constantly vigilant against any threat to its carefully constructed self-image.

Pride manifests in this hypersensitivity through:

- Interpreting neutral comments as personal attacks

- Assuming negative intentions behind ambiguous actions

- Deflecting responsibility when mistakes occur

- Nursing grievances long after others have forgotten the incident

- Mounting elaborate defenses against even constructive feedback

- Finding forgiveness nearly impossible when feeling disrespected

"For where jealousy and selfish ambition exist, there will be disorder and every vile practice." (James 3:16) This ancient observation captures the relational chaos that follows when pride's quick offense drives our interactions. What might have been minor disagreements escalate into bitter conflicts; potential collaborations dissolve into competition; communities fragment into factions all because pride cannot bear the weight of a perceived slight.

DEAL WITH PRIDE

Address pride before pride addresses you—often through painful lessons and lost opportunities. The antidote to pride isn't self-hatred but humility, that misunderstood virtue that represents not weakness but strength.

Humility remains unique among virtues in that it cannot be achieved through direct pursuit. The moment you believe you've attained humility is the moment you've lost

OFFENSE

it. It develops instead through practice and perspective, cultivated through daily choices that gradually reshape our character.

"Humble yourselves under the mighty hand of God, that He may exalt you in due time, casting all your care upon Him, for He cares for you." (1 Peter 5:6-7)

This passage intertwines two spiritual practices that, performed together, form humility's foundation. First comes the deliberate placement of ourselves "under the mighty hand of God"—an acknowledgment of a power and wisdom beyond our own. This isn't groveling self-abasement but the recognition of proper order and proportion, seeing ourselves accurately within a larger reality.

The promise that follows"that He may exalt you in due time"—reveals humility's paradox. True elevation comes not through self-promotion but through the recognition of proper time and sequence. Not "if" but "when," not through striving but through waiting. This requires the patience born of trust, the willingness to allow proper timing rather than demanding immediate recognition.

The second practice—"casting all your care upon Him, for He cares for you"—connects humility with surrender. Pride manifests as the determination to

176

control our circumstances, to bear our own burdens, to need no one. Humility acknowledges interdependence and accepts help. The justification for this vulnerability lies not in our inadequacy but in God's character—"for He cares for you." We can release our white-knuckled grip precisely because we are valued.

Here we discover the beautiful synthesis: humility and trust reinforce each other. Humility creates space for trust, and trust nurtures humility. The mighty hand under which we humble ourselves is the same hand that carries our concerns with tender care.

THE POSTURE OF HUMILITY

Ancient text records one of history's most potent demonstrations of humility:

"And Jacob lifted up his eyes and looked, and behold, Esau came, and with him four hundred men... He passed over before them and bowed himself to the ground seven times until he came near to his brother."

The scene captures a pivotal moment between estranged brothers, Jacob, who had stolen his brother's birthright through deception, now approaching Esau, who had vowed revenge. What makes this encounter remarkable is Jacob's approach: seven deliberate acts of prostration, each communicating profound deference.

In ancient Near Eastern culture, the symbolism was unmistakable. Seven represented completeness and perfection. To bow seven times signified total submission, the posture of servant to master. Consider what made this extraordinary: Jacob, not Esau, possessed the paternal blessing. Jacob, not Esau, had received divine promises. By all spiritual metrics, Jacob held the superior position.

Yet here was the blessed one, taking the posture of a servant.

This wasn't merely strategic self-abasement to avoid conflict. Jacob had been transformed by his own encounter with the divine, famously wrestling until daybreak and receiving both blessing and wound. True humility is often born this way—through struggle, through recognition of our limitations, through encounter with something greater than ourselves.

The irony resonates across millennia: "He who wants to be the greatest must be the least, and he who wants to be the master must also be the servant of all." Jacob embodied this paradox before it was articulated, demonstrating that genuine strength is revealed not in domination but in the willingness to bend low.

True humility remains elusive precisely because it cannot be manufactured or performed. It emerges only through genuine transformation, when our perception of ourselves and others has been fundamentally altered. Those who merely act humble while harboring pride engage in the most dangerous form of deception—self-deception.

The invitation stands: Humble yourself under the mighty hand of God. This is not something others can do for you, nor something God will force upon you. It requires choice, action, behavior—a daily decision to live with accurate self-perception. The alternative carries its own warning: humbling that comes not as gentle guidance but as necessary correction.

You stand at the crossroads of pride and humility. Choose wisely, recognizing that the path downward is, paradoxically, the path upward—and the mighty hand under which you bow is the same hand that will lift you in due time.

Chapter 18

CHURCH HURT: THE SILENT EPIDEMIC

UNDERSTANDING THE WOUND

Church hurt is the profound emotional and spiritual trauma that occurs within what should be our safest sanctuary. It's the bewildering pain of being wounded in the house of a friend, as the prophet Zechariah might describe it. This injury strikes at our most vulnerable core—our faith journey and relationship with the Divine.

When we experience church hurt, we suffer not merely from interpersonal conflict, but from a spiritual dissonance that can shake our very foundations. The place designed to nurture and protect becomes the source of our deepest wounds. The shepherds called to tend become the wolves who scatter. The family meant to embrace becomes the tribe that excludes.

Research from the Hartford Institute for Religion Research reveals the sobering reality: approximately 40% of those who abandon their church communities cite relational conflict as the primary catalyst. Another 18% point to emotional or spiritual abuse, while 27% leave because of leadership conflicts. These aren't merely statistics, they represent souls in crisis, faith journeys interrupted, and spiritual homes abandoned.

What makes church hurt particularly insidious is that it often comes disguised in spiritual language and cloaked in divine authority. The very scriptures meant to liberate become chains that bind. The cross intended for salvation becomes a sword that divides. And God's name, which should inspire love, becomes weaponized to instill fear and compliance.

Yet we must acknowledge an uncomfortable truth: not all Church hurt stems from malicious intent. Many wounds result from careless words, thoughtless actions, or systemic failures born of human limitation rather than calculated cruelty. The church, after all, remains a collection of imperfect beings struggling to reflect a perfect God. As James reminds us, we all stumble in many ways (James 3:2).

The consequences of church hurt extend far beyond momentary discomfort. For many, it triggers a cascade of spiritual crises: doubt that undermines certainty, bitterness that poisons joy, disengagement that replaces commitment, and in countless cases, a wholesale abandonment of organized faith. The very institution designed to foster spiritual growth becomes, paradoxically, the greatest obstacle to it.

THE MEMBER'S MIRROR: HOW WE WOUND ONE ANOTHER

The church's tapestry is woven with threads of diverse personalities, backgrounds, and spiritual maturity. This beautiful diversity can also become the source of profound friction when we forget our common purpose.

Some members carry with them a critical spirit that poisons the well of fellowship. They approach church not as grateful participants but as demanding consumers, armed with complaint rather than contribution. Paul's exhortation to "do all things without complaining and disputing" (Philippians 2:14) falls on deaf ears as they spread their discontent like a contagion throughout the body.

Gossip—that seemingly innocent exchange of information—becomes a weapon of mass destruction in church communities. What begins as "prayer requests" transforms into character assassination. What starts as "concerns" evolves into campaigns of whispered destruction. Solomon's wisdom pierces through our justifications: "A perverse person stirs up conflict, and a gossip separates close friends" (Proverbs 16:28). With each careless word, we drive wedges between brothers and sisters, creating factions where there should be family.

Pride manifests in subtle yet devastating ways among church members. Like the Pharisee who "trusted in himself that he was righteous and despised others" (Luke 18:9), we establish ourselves as the arbiters of authentic faith. We create hierarchies of holiness, measuring others against our self-designed standards. The "right" way to worship, dress, speak, or serve becomes our litmus test for genuine Christianity, turning the church from a hospital for sinners into a museum for saints.

Jealousy and envy corrupt our ability to celebrate the diverse gifts within the body. When another's ministry flourishes, when another's testimony inspires, when another's service receives recognition, our congratulations come through gritted teeth. We forget Paul's teaching that "there are different kinds of gifts, but the same Spirit distributes them" (1 Corinthians 12:4), and that every part of the body is essential, regardless of its visibility or acclaim.

Our actions speak even louder than our attitudes. We form exclusive cliques that contradict Paul's plea in 1 Corinthians 1:10 that *"there be no divisions among you." We reject biblical authority when it challenges our preferences, ignoring the admonition to "obey those who rule over you" (Hebrews 13:17). We import worldly values, practices, and priorities into church life, forgetting that "friendship with the world is enmity with God"* (James 4:4).

Perhaps most damaging is our reluctance to forgive. We cling to offenses like precious jewelry, polishing our grievances until they shine brightly enough for all to see. We disregard Jesus' teaching on unlimited forgiveness in Matthew 18:21-35, preferring instead the temporary satisfaction of justified resentment. In doing so, we become chained to our offenders, dragged down by the very wounds we refuse to release.

Our relationships suffer as we judge harshly rather than love lavishly. We speak evil of fellow believers, damaging reputations and destroying trust, despite James' clear command: *"Do not speak evil of one another, brethren"* (James 4:11). We neglect our call to "endeavor to keep the unity of the Spirit in the bond of peace" (Ephesians 4:3), allowing petty differences to create chasms of division.

Even in worship, we think primarily of ourselves rather than the community. Like the Corinthian church (1

Corinthians 11:17-22), we bring disruptive attitudes and selfish ambitions to what should be sacred gatherings. We fail to consider how our expressions of worship might impact others, forgetting Paul's instruction not to *"put a stumbling block or a cause to fall in our brother's way"* (Romans 14:13).

At its core, this member-to-member wounding reflects our forgetfulness of our true identity as "members of one body" (1 Corinthians 12:12-27). When we wound one another, we ultimately wound ourselves. When we divide the body, we diminish its effectiveness. When we fracture fellowship, we frustrate God's purpose for His church.

LEADERSHIP'S SHADOW: THE ABUSE OF SACRED TRUST

Perhaps no church hurt cuts deeper than that inflicted by those entrusted with spiritual care. When shepherds wound their sheep, the damage extends beyond the individual to the very concept of spiritual authority itself.

The corruption of leadership begins when position becomes a platform for self-importance rather than service. Jesus modeled servant leadership by washing His disciples' feet, yet many leaders today prefer to be served than to serve. They "lord their authority over others" (1 Peter 5:3), creating resentment rather than respect, fear rather than love. They drag struggling members deeper into pain, demanding healing without offering help, expecting growth without providing nurture.

Pride manifests in leadership through an unteachable spirit that rejects correction and accountability. Such leaders consider themselves beyond question, their decisions beyond scrutiny, their authority beyond challenge. When criticism comes, they label it rebellion; when questions arise, they call it disrespect; when accountability is suggested, they denounce it as undermining authority.

Among the most devastating forms of leadership abuse is the weaponization of the pulpit. Rather than following Jesus' teaching on personal reconciliation (Matthew 18:15-17), some leaders use their platform to launch public attacks against members who cannot respond. Instead of picking up the phone, scheduling a meeting, or making a home visit to understand a situation, they fire salvos from the safety of the pulpit, settling scores under the guise of preaching truth. This violation of sacred trust turns the platform of proclamation into a battleground of personal vendettas.

Even more insidious is the manipulation of spiritual language and scripture to justify personal agendas. God's

Word becomes twisted to support human preferences. Divine authority becomes conflated with opinion. "God told me" becomes the conversation-ending trump card that brooks no opposition. This misrepresentation of God's character and intentions creates not just interpersonal wounds but spiritual trauma, as people struggle to distinguish between the true voice of the Shepherd and its human counterfeit.

The misuse of scripture compounds this damage. Verses plucked from context become bludgeons rather than balm. The Bible, meant to be bread that nourishes, becomes a brick that bruises. Leaders selectively apply passages that reinforce their authority while conveniently ignoring those that address their responsibility.

Perhaps most hypocritical is the leadership that preaches Christ's humility while refusing to embody it. Such leaders maintain emotional and spiritual distance from their congregants, positioning themselves above the flock rather than among it. They demand submission without offering support, expect loyalty without demonstrating love, require vulnerability without reciprocating it. This stark contrast between proclaimed values and reality creates deep cynicism about both the messenger and the message.

Jesus' model of leadership offers a radically different paradigm: "Whoever wants to become great among you must be your servant, and whoever wants to be first must be slave of all. For even the Son of Man did not come to be served, but to serve, and to give his life as a ransom for many" (Mark 10:43-45). True spiritual authority flows from sacrificial service, not positional power. A faithful shepherd, like Jesus, willingly bends down to carry the wounded, takes time for personal connection, and creates spaces for honest dialogue.

Leaders must never forget that they will one day give an account to God for how they shepherded His flock (Hebrews 13:17). Their voice, their authority, their influence are borrowed, not owned; entrusted, not deserved; given for others' benefit, not personal advantage.

HEALING THE WOUNDS: A PATHWAY FORWARD

While complete elimination of church hurt remains impossible in communities of imperfect people, intentional efforts can significantly reduce its frequency and impact. The path forward requires commitment from both leadership and membership to create environments where healing outpaces harm.

CREATING ACCOUNTABILITY SYSTEMS AND TRANSPARENCY

Healthy churches establish clear, accessible procedures for addressing concerns and resolving conflicts. These aren't merely documents gathering dust on a shelf but living processes known and trusted by the congregation. Designated individuals—respected for their wisdom and impartiality—must be available to hear concerns without default defensiveness or dismissal.

External oversight provides crucial perspective that internal dynamics often miss. Regular audits of church culture, leadership practices, and conflict resolution patterns by qualified outside observers can identify troubling trends before they become toxic patterns. Transparency in decision-making processes, financial management, and policy development builds trust by eliminating the secrecy that so often breeds suspicion.

The transparent church operates not in fear of exposure but in confidence of integrity. As Jesus taught, "For there is nothing hidden that will not be disclosed, and nothing concealed that will not be known or brought out into the open" (Luke 8:17). Embracing this reality proactively rather than reactively demonstrates a commitment to truth that transcends image management.

IMPROVING LEADERSHIP DEVELOPMENT AND TRAINING

Spiritual authority without emotional intelligence creates battlefields instead of sanctuaries. Leaders must be trained not just in biblical knowledge but in recognizing and managing their own emotional triggers, understanding power dynamics, practicing empathetic listening, and implementing trauma-informed approaches to ministry.

Leadership development must include comprehensive education in recognizing and addressing various forms of spiritual abuse. Many leaders perpetuate harmful patterns not from malice but from ignorance, repeating what they experienced without examining its impact. Breaking these cycles requires conscious education about healthy and unhealthy uses of spiritual authority.

Healthy succession planning prevents the concentration of power that often leads to abuse. Churches that intentionally develop multiple leaders, distribute authority appropriately, and plan thoughtfully for leadership transitions create stability that survives individual personalities. As Paul instructed Timothy, *"The things you have heard me say in the presence of many witnesses entrust to reliable people who will also be qualified to teach others"* (2 Timothy 2:2).

FOSTERING AUTHENTIC COMMUNITY

Safe spaces for sharing struggles without fear of judgment form the foundation of authentic community. These might be small groups where genuine relationships develop, recovery ministries where brokenness is acknowledged rather than hidden, or mentoring relationships where vulnerability is met with wisdom rather than criticism.

Communities that make room for questions and doubts demonstrate intellectual and spiritual humility. They recognize that faith journeys include seasons of certainty and uncertainty, and that honest wrestling often produces deeper conviction than unexamined acceptance. As one psalmist modeled, authentic faith can include both desperate questions and determined trust.

Support systems that extend beyond Sunday services acknowledge that life's challenges don't observe a weekly schedule. Prayer chains, meal deliveries, childcare assistance, counseling referrals, and practical help during crises demonstrate love in action rather than merely in proclamation. As James reminds us, *"Suppose a brother or a sister is without clothes and daily food. If one of you says to them, 'Go in peace; keep warm and well fed,' but does nothing about their physical needs, what good is it?"* (James 2:15-16).

IMPLEMENTING PROPER BOUNDARIES

Clearly defined roles for staff and volunteers prevent the confusion and conflict that arise from ambiguous expectations. Written policies regarding appropriate behavior, relationships, and communication create protective parameters that benefit everyone involved. Regular review of decision-making processes ensures that proper checks and balances remain in place, particularly regarding financial matters, staff supervision, and program implementation.

Special attention must be given to protecting vulnerable populations within the congregation. Children, elderly members, those with disabilities, those experiencing financial hardship, and those in emotional crisis all require particular care to ensure their vulnerability isn't exploited, intentionally or unintentionally.

As Paul advised in Romans 12:10, "Be devoted to one another in love. Honor one another above yourselves." This devotion includes protecting one another through thoughtful boundaries that acknowledge human weakness while facilitating genuine connection.

PRIORITIZING HEALING AND RECONCILIATION

Churches serious about addressing hurt must have trained counselors available or maintain strong referral networks for professional help. Some wounds require expertise beyond what well-meaning pastoral care can provide. Recognizing these limitations doesn't diminish spiritual authority but demonstrates wise stewardship of souls.

Processes for addressing past hurts must be established before they're needed. These include mechanisms for acknowledging harm done, offering genuine apologies (not the non-apology of "I'm sorry if you were offended"), and making meaningful amends where possible. Jesus' teaching in Matthew 5:23-24 places reconciliation even above worship: "If you are offering your gift at the altar and there remember that your brother or sister has something against you, leave your gift there in front of the altar. First go and be reconciled to them; then come and offer your gift."

Prioritizing healing means creating space for lament as well as praise, for grief as well as celebration, for honest processing as well as forward movement. It means acknowledging that spiritual growth often occurs through, not despite, our deepest wounds. As the psalmist testified, *"Before I was afflicted, I went astray, but now I obey your word"* (Psalm 119:67).

THE CHURCH REIMAGINED

The church was never meant to be perfect—it was meant to be transformative. Its power lies not in flawless performance but in an authentic community where imperfect people experience perfect love. When we acknowledge our capacity to wound one another, implement safeguards against the most damaging behaviors, and create pathways for genuine healing, we don't diminish the church's testimony—we strengthen it.

A church that can honestly confront its failures while faithfully pursuing its calling offers the world something far more compelling than pretended perfection. It demonstrates the very essence of the gospel: that grace transforms, that reconciliation is possible, that love indeed "covers over a multitude of sins" (1 Peter 4:8).

In such a community, church hurt doesn't have the final word. It becomes instead the starting point for deeper understanding, more authentic relationships, and renewed commitment to reflecting Christ to a world desperate for genuine hope. This is the church reimagined. Not as an institution immune to hurt, but as a family resilient enough to heal.

CONCLUSION

Writing this book about offense has been an unexpected journey for me. I hope it has taken you on a meaningful adventure, unraveling a topic that has, and will affect every individual at one point in their lives. It brings me great joy to imagine Jesus nodding in approval and saying, "Well done, Ebo, for sharing My heart with the world."

This book was born out of personal experiences with offense that challenged my walk with God. In 2024, I realized that if I didn't address offense in my life, it would jeopardize my relationship with Him. I sought the Lord in pain, tears, and sleepless nights, and He answered me. He revealed how offense has marred countless relationships and driven a wedge among His children. It hardens hearts, closes the heavens, extinguishes spiritual fervor, and chills the fire of prayer.

The burden of writing this book was heavy, but as I embraced it, I understood the scripture: *"My yoke is easy, and My burden is light."* God guided my thoughts and inspired me, even interrupting my sleep to pour out insights.

I pray that God touches your heart and heal any lingering pain. I ask that anyone under the bondage of offense be loosed now. May the light of God shine on you and cause you to see the manipulations of the devil that have kept you bound. Your Father desires to rescue, redeem, and heal you. May God compensate you for all that you have lost. May the spirit of humility rest on us and in us. May the influence of self be broken over our lives. I declare that from today, you have received wisdom to navigate the attack of offense. I declare that from today, you will not be sensitive to the things of the flesh. I declare in the name of Jesus that your healing begins now and it is complete. Unnecessary anger is done away with in Jesus' name.

I leave you with these scriptures:

"Great peace have they which love thy law: and nothing shall offend them." - Psalm 119:165.

I pray that we will get to the place where nothing offends us.

"And herein do I exercise myself, to have always a conscience void of offense toward God, and toward men." - Acts 24:16.

And finally, may we never get to this point:

"And then shall many be offended, and shall betray one another, and shall hate one another." -Matthew 24:10.

May God bless you, your family, your church, and all that is yours.

www.ingramcontent.com/pod-product-compliance
Lightning Source LLC
LaVergne TN
LVHW051231080426
835513LV00016B/1526